WHAT
DOES
THIS
MEAN?

WHAT DOES THIS MEAN?

LUTHER'S CATECHISMS TODAY

Edited by Phillip E. Pederson

AUGSBURG Publishing House • Minneapolis

WHAT DOES THIS MEAN?

ABOUT THE COVER

The illustration on the cover of this book depicts the "Luther rose," an emblem Martin Luther developed from his family coat of arms and interpreted as a symbol of his theology. Some of the themes he saw in the emblem were faith in the crucified Christ, the fruits of faith, and the joy and bliss of the world to come already beginning to transform life on earth.

CONTENTS

INTRODUCTION

INTRODUCTION

Almost 500 years ago, Martin Luther was captured by the gospel. That gracious captivity freed him, and he then proceeded to set the gospel free in the world.

Before Luther, through a process that had been going on for centuries, the message of God's grace in Jesus Christ toward humankind had become so blurred that its liberating sound could not be heard. It had become encrusted with church regulations, distorted by pious myths and human ceremonials, abused by human greed, and buried under theological jargon. However, the grace of God set the mind and heart of Martin Luther free. He, in turn, set the gospel message free and made it sing.

It did not happen without a struggle. For Luther, it meant disappointing his father's dreams that he become a lawyer; it meant a frustrating search through the harsh discipline of monastic life for an inner peace that eluded him even there; it meant intense study and hard work; it meant taking on the responsibility of teaching the Bible in a new and remote university; it meant throwing off the weight of centuries of religious tradition; and it meant a direct confrontation with the magisterial teaching authority of the medieval church. Above all, it meant total honesty with God and with himself.

Somehow Luther thrived on the struggle. Through it he found new vitality. His zest for living showed in his teaching and preaching, in his debates with opponents of all kinds from all over Europe, in his fresh and down-to-earth writing, and in his love for his family and human companionship. A warm humanity pervaded his speech, his actions, and his relationships with everyone he met or dealt with. Certainly his struggle made him a man of integrity. He had struggled with God and with his own conscience. After that, he was ready to defy an emperor to his face and a pope in imperial Rome. When such a man has the ability to tell his story in words that compel us to live with him through it all, and to write about the gospel with a vitality that reflects the power of the biblical narrative itself, then we begin to un-

11

12   INTRODUCTION

derstand how he carried half a continent with him in his lifetime. No
wonder he continues to fascinate us and grip our attention after more
than four and a half centuries.

Yet the current lively interest in Luther would not be possible except for intense scholarly efforts over the past 150 years to recover
the literary remains of his active life and vast work. A long line of
competent and dedicated scholars have worked diligently at this
task. The success of their long search has now culminated, for the
English-speaking world, in the publication of the 55-volume American
Edition of *Luther's Works.*[1] This enterprise, lasting over 20 years and
translating the most significant of Luther's writings, was completed in
1976. At last we have in our hands a resource which makes it possible for us to discover for ourselves the richness of religious wisdom
and evangelical insight which is Luther's legacy to the church, to the
world, and to us.

All of this is most welcome to Lutheran Christians, who have known
for a long time that Luther was a superb teacher, capable of expressing the most profound theological insight in language that could
move and instruct both children and adults. One of the finest examples of his gifts as a religious writer is his *Small Catechism.* Most
Lutherans have known it simply as "the Catechism." Sometimes
they have taken for granted the value of this little booklet, and yet
450 years after its first publication it continues to teach, inspire, and
comfort thousands of young people and adults through its simple—
almost childlike, yet also profound—grasp of the Christian faith.

Unfortunately, the majority of Lutherans, including some who
know the *Small Catechism* best, are unaware that this booklet has a
companion piece, also by Luther, with equally helpful insight into the
chief elements of Christian faith. This other book, far larger in size,
is called the *Large Catechism.* The writing and preparation for both
catechisms was underway at about the same time, so that while they
differ in style, what is expressed in one finds its echo in the other.
While Lutheran pastors have always known of its existence, the
Large Catechism has not been used nearly as much as its smaller partner. Consequently its value has not been recognized nearly as widely.

Presenting both catechisms together in a single volume enables us
to recover for our own generation the resources for worship, private
prayer, understanding and insight, and consolation which they contain. By printing each commandment, each article of the Creed, and
each petition of the Lord's Prayer from one catechism with its companion from the other, Luther's *Large Catechism* can become the

[1] Martin Luther, *Luther's Works,* Jaroslav Pelikan and Helmut T. Lehmann,
eds., 55 vols. (Philadelphia: Fortress, 1955-76). Hereafter cited as *LW.*

teaching and interpretive partner of the *Small Catechism*, and thereby enrich the use of both.

It is anticipated that the primary use of this publication will be as an aid for those who teach the catechisms to confirmation or other Christian instruction classes. It is also expected that this book will prove its value in a wider circle. It creates a new resource on which pastors can draw for their preaching and teaching ministries. Parents, whom Luther intended to be the primary teachers of the *Small Catechism* to their families, will find it a helpful guide for religious development in their homes. Parish education committees who encourage their teaching staffs to become acquainted with its contents will be promoting the development of new and fresh uses of the catechisms to enliven Christian education programs.

What follows is a three-part introduction to assist the reader to make the most profitable use of these texts. The first part tells the story of how the catechisms arose: Luther's frustrations with the spiritual condition of the church of his own time; the woeful lack of even the most elementary understanding of the Christian faith; his early attempts to provide spiritual direction for his "beloved Germans;" and finally the writing of the works themselves. The second part deals with the subsequent use of the catechisms, the impact they have had on the life of the church, and the significance they have had beyond the Reformation period and outside Reformation lands. Finally, we offer some suggestions about the use of the catechisms for instructional purposes. It is the hope of those who have planned this volume that these suggestions will stimulate the thinking of all who teach—that they may apply the best of their training and experience to finding imaginative and exciting ways to help their students, of whatever age, discover and make their own these excellent resources for Christian faith and life.

I

THE STORY BEHIND
THE CATECHISMS

Martin Luther did not invent the catechetical method of Christian instruction. Neither was he the first to provide an explanation for children and for the common people of the Ten Commandments, the Apostles' Creed, or the Lord's Prayer. A long catechetical tradition has been traced back at least three centuries before Luther first began to deal with these subjects, and the question-and-answer pattern for teaching can be found in the 8th and 9th centuries. Knowledge of the Commandments, the Creed, and the Lord's Prayer had been expected of Christian people for a long time. However, in Luther's day it was clear that vast numbers of both clergy and lay people had no real understanding of these most basic elements of Christian faith and religious practice.

In 1531, as Luther looked back on the situation he had found in the churches of Saxony, he described it in these words: "No one knew the real meaning of the gospel, Christ, baptism, confession, the sacrament of the altar, faith, Spirit, flesh, good works, the Ten Commandments, the Our Father, prayer, suffering, comfort, temporal government, the state of matrimony, parents, children, masters, manservant, mistress, maidservant, devils, angels, world, life, death, sin, justice, forgiveness, God, bishop, pastor, church, a Christian, or the cross. In brief, we were totally ignorant about all that it is necessary for a Christian to know." [2]

This deplorable state of religious life in Germany was attributed to a number of causes, including poor training for the clergy, lack of pastoral concern in the upper levels of church administration (among the bishops and popes), and a widespread deterioration of morality. All of this contrasted sharply with Luther's notion of what the church should be like and how it should be cared for. In his capacity as professor of biblical studies at the University of Wittenberg he was

[2] From "Dr. Martin Luther's Warning to His Dear German People," *LW*, vol. 47, p. 52. See also a similar statement cited by Theodore Graebner in *The Story of the Catechism* (St. Louis: Concordia, 1928), p. 9.

required to probe the Scriptures. There he discovered a profound grasp of the reality and totality of sin, both in individual human lives and in all the institutions humans devise for ordering society. But alongside that discovery he found another, namely the unconditional grace and mercy of God given through Jesus Christ, who had overcome the powers of sin and broken their grip. Through his cross, Christ had become the Savior of sinners and the source of a new love in their lives. Out of the Bible's proclamation of these themes came Luther's doctrine of justification by faith alone, through grace alone. This doctrine gave him an entirely new view of what the Bible was about and became the focal point of all his teaching and preaching. He called this doctrine "our gospel," and from it all evangelical churches were, in time, to draw their strength. However, all of this took time to develop.

The first public opportunity for Luther to deal with the condition of the churches came in the summer of 1516, when he temporarily took the place of Simon Heinz as preacher for the city church in Wittenberg, across town from the more famous Castle Church of the Elector. During that fall and until the following February Luther preached a series of sermons on the Ten Commandments. Almost immediately upon completing this series, he began to preach a Lenten cycle of sermons on the Lord's Prayer. From these early sermonic beginnings there developed in his mind an increasingly clear outline of what was needed for effective religious instruction in the churches. Later in 1517 he produced a small tract explaining the Ten Commandments, to help members of the Wittenberg parish church prepare themselves for Holy Communion. In that tract he discussed confession of sins in the traditional language of repentance or penance; but he also began to move beyond descriptions of specific sins to explanations about the nature of sin itself. (In the fall of that same year Luther attacked the practice of indulgences, which he regarded as an abuse of the church's sacrament of penance, or confession. The publication at the end of October, 1517 of his *Ninety-Five Theses* attacking indulgences was the act with which the Reformation, as an historic movement, began.) Luther also began to write about the larger commandment of love which lay beneath every specific commandment. These changes were in line with his new evangelical understanding of the Scriptures. In addition, it is likely that he had these instructions printed as posters or placards, a fairly common practice at that time, so they would be easily accessible to all who came to church. For a broader reading public, Luther also revised his sermons of 1516 and 1517 on the Ten Commandments and had them published in book form in 1518. The following year, 1519, he also published his sermons on the Lord's Prayer. Two supplementary tracts on prayer also appeared from his pen. These writings were enthusiastically received in Germany and beyond. Luther was awakening powerful religious impulses through these booklets, along with his other writings. His readers were being moved.[3]

The climax of this first period of Luther's catechetical labors was the publication in 1520—the same year he published his most influential treatises for the reform of the church—of *A Short Form of the Ten Commandments, a Short Form of the Creed, and a Short Form of the Lord's Prayer*. This *Short Form* handbook with the long title was the forerunner of the *Small Catechism*. Luther's clarity of language and lively grasp of the gospel brought immediate acclaim for this work. Moreover, the order in which the chief parts were arranged—Commandments, followed by the Creed, followed by the Lord's Prayer—was specifically cited by Luther as important in itself for a correct understanding of the relationship between God's law and his gospel. Luther wrote that first the Ten Commandments teach a person "what he can do and what he cannot do, what he can avoid and what he cannot avoid, with the result that he recognizes himself as a sinful and wicked man." Then "the Creed offers grace as a remedy" and "reveals God and his mercy." Finally, the Lord's Prayer instructs the person "how to desire and seek this grace, and shows how to secure it." [4] After 1520, Luther never departed from this order in the catechetical materials he produced. In 1522, the *Short Form* was reissued under the title *Booklet of Prayers*, and contained additional explanations of the "Hail Mary" and the epistle to Titus, together with prayers based on eight psalms.

After his dramatic hearing before Emperor Charles V at Worms in April, 1521, and his subsequent "exile" in the Wartburg Castle not far from Eisenach, Luther was recalled to Wittenberg in March of 1522 and resumed his regular duties. At this time he began a new series of sermons on the three chief parts, which he increasingly referred to collectively as "the catechism." The following year he preached another round of sermons on the same topics in the parish church. His successor there, Johann Bugenhagen, continued this

[3] M. Reu, *Dr. Martin Luther's Small Catechism: A History of Its Origin, Its Distribution and Its Use* (Chicago: Wartburg Publishing House, 1929), has been a major source of information for the historical section of this introduction. Dr. Reu's work, in turn, reflects the research of O. Albrecht, editor of vol. 30, part 1, of the authoritative Weimar Edition of *D. Martin Luthers Werke: Kritische Gesamtausgabe* (Weimar: Hermann Böhlaus Nachfolger, 1910). Additional helpful material is given in Carl Volz, ed., *Teaching the Faith: Luther's Catechisms in Perspective* (River Forest, Illinois: Lutheran Education Association, 1976).

[4] John Nicholas Lenker, ed., *Luther on Christian Education*, vol. 1 (Minneapolis: The Luther Press, 1907), p. 192.

practice, and in time most Lutheran churches in Germany made this a regular procedure.

In 1524 Luther's young colleague at Wittenberg, Philip Melanchthon, prepared the first of two catechisms he was to publish. The second appeared four years later. In 1525 Luther asked two fellow reformers, Justus Jonas and Johann Schneider (better known as Johann Agricola), to put their hands to the same task because of the immense need for materials with which to instruct the people. Luther first began to use the term *catechism* in the sense of a book at this time. These two friends did not publish anything of this nature, but that year a handbook, *Booklet for Laymen and Children* (probably by Bugenhagen), was published. It is similar in many respects to what Luther had already issued. A new feature was the addition of explanations on Baptism and the Lord's Supper.

During the years 1522 to 1529, approximately 30 catechisms appeared in Germany. One of these, published in 1523 by Urbanus Rhegius (a reformer in the city of Augsburg), proposed changing the customary catechetical style and having the children ask questions of a parent or teacher, who would then provide the answers. Another catechism, written by Johann Brenz of Württemberg in 1527, provided two sets of questions, one for younger and one for older children. Brenz' catechism enjoyed wide popularity, especially in southern Germany, where it was circulated along with Luther's catechisms for many years.

Meanwhile Luther became involved in the broader scope of Christian education. In 1524 he wrote a treatise for the city councilmen of Germany urging the establishment of public education for all children, both boys and girls. In this recommendation he urged that basic instruction in the fundamentals of the Christian faith be included. When in 1527 the Elector of Saxony was organizing a program of visitations to all the parishes of his realm, to be conducted by teams of two theologians and two court officials, Melanchthon was instructed to write his *Instructions for Visitors*. Luther worked closely with him in preparation of these guidelines for the life of the congregations of Saxony. When it appeared in 1528, one section of the *Instructions* recommended that sermons on the catechism be preached each Sunday afternoon, followed by recitation of the chief parts by the children. In November of that year, and possibly later, Luther participated in these visitations himself and was appalled by the conditions he found existing in the churches. The situation was even worse than he had anticipated. Many of the parish pastors were poorly equipped to preach or teach, and were abysmally ignorant about the Bible. As a result, members of these parishes were barely aware of even the most elementary teachings of Christianity and were filled with superstitious notions. Luther returned from these visits even more determined than ever to overcome this ignorance and to change the character of religious life among his people.

In the spring of 1528 Bugenhagen had left Wittenberg to carry out the Lutheran reform in Brunswick, so Luther again returned to the pulpit in the town church. In May he preached a series of sermons on the parts of the catechism and in September offered a second series. By October he had begun work on a printed volume containing somewhat lengthy explanations of the catechism. These were based on the sermons he had recently been preaching but also reached back to materials used in the *Short Form* he had developed at the beginning of the decade. This work was interrupted by his participation in the visitations during November. On his return to Wittenberg, he resumed both his writing and preaching with a new sense of urgency in light of the conditions he had witnessed in the churches throughout the territory. On the completion of this third set of sermons, he undertook a new project to supplement the work still in progress.

By January of 1529 Luther had prepared a new set of charts or posters which provided concise, clear explanations of the first three chief parts of the catechism—the Ten Commandments, the Apostles' Creed, and the Lord's Prayer. By the middle of March of that same year a second set of charts appeared dealing with the two sacraments of Baptism and the Lord's Supper. This was followed soon after, perhaps in the same month, by a third set containing table prayers, prayers for morning and evening, and a series of Bible quotations outlining the duties of householders, parents, children, rulers and the like. In Hamburg, Bugenhagen was so delighted with the charts—they were just what he needed to reorganize the churches there—that he had them printed in book form in Low German, the dialect spoken in those regions.

At the same time that these charts were being rushed through the printers' shops, Luther continued to work on the longer explanations he had begun the previous fall. This work was finally completed and published in April, 1529, under the title *The German Catechism of Martin Luther*. It contained the texts of the Ten Commandments, the Apostles' Creed, the Lord's Prayer, the biblical passages associated with Baptism and the Lord's Supper, and rather detailed explanations of those texts. A second edition later in the year contained an addition to the explanation of the Lord's Prayer—dealing with the opening address of the prayer—and an exhortation to confession of sins before Holy Communion. A third edition in 1530 added the longer preface now usually printed with this work. Today we know this *German Catechism* as Luther's *Large Catechism*. At the time of its publication, its smaller partner had not yet come into existence as a book, so the latter title appeared only after the *Small Catechism* had become well-known.

The *Large Catechism,* which was the outgrowth of a long period of preaching by Luther on the parts of the catechism, was especially useful to pastors. Not only did it provide helpful explanations and useful illustrations of the biblical materials, which the pastors could apply in whatever instruction they provided for the children of their parishes, but also it was arranged in a style ready-made for pulpit use. Parts of this book were often read from pulpits in place of original sermons. It soon became the basic commentary employed by Lutheran clergy for their catechetical work.

While all this was going on, Luther was also at work on a book edition of the material produced earlier on the three sets of charts. Finally, on May 16, 1529, the *Small Catechism* was published. This is its birthdate. The book contained the five chief parts as we know them today, with their accompanying explanations, together with the "Table Prayers," the "Morning and Evening Prayers," and the "Table of Duties" that appeared on the second and third set of charts. In addition, a section called the "Marriage Booklet" was included. Unfortunately, no copies of this first edition survive, but the makeup of the original is known from three copies of reprints made later. A second edition was published within a month, but all traces of it have disappeared. A third edition issued on June 13, 1529, carried the title *Enchiridion* (*Handbook*) and an added "Baptism Booklet," "Short Form of Confession," a German liturgy with musical notations, and three collects (liturgical prayers). These additional elements provided a valuable "additional services book" for pastors and church members. Subsequent editions often included liturgical additions supplied by their editors.

In 1531 Luther published the *Small Catechism* in the final form he was to give to it personally. The only new item was his excellent explanation of the introductory words of address of the Lord's Prayer. The "Short Form of Confession" from the June 13, 1529, edition was revised and relocated following the section on Baptism. The seven reprintings of this book which appeared before Luther's death in February, 1546, contained only minor verbal changes, concerned mostly with bringing biblical quotations into agreement with Luther's 1534 translation of the Bible. Ten other editions were printed elsewhere in Germany before Luther's death.

Two notable additions to Luther's text did not originate with him and appeared just shortly after his death. One is the "Office of the Keys" and the other is the "Christian Questions" for those about to receive the Lord's Supper. The former probably originated with the *Nürnberg Sermons for Children* of 1533. This book was an expansion

of Luther's *Small Catechism,* and enjoyed wide circulation and a good
reputation in Germany and beyond for many years.

With the completion of the *Small Catechism,* Luther presented it to
his people with the following preface, revealing his motivation for this
effort: "The deplorable conditions which I recently encountered when
I was a visitor constrained me to prepare this brief and simple catechism or statement of Christian teaching. Good God, what wretchedness I beheld! The common people, especially those who live in the
country, have no knowledge whatever of Christian teaching, and unfortunately many pastors are quite incompetent and unfitted for
teaching. Although the people are supposed to be Christian, are baptized, and receive the holy sacrament, they do not know the Lord's
Prayer, the Creed, or the Ten Commandments, they live as if they
were pigs and irrational beasts, and now that the Gospel has been
restored they have mastered the fine art of abusing liberty." [5] (The
concluding phrase is a reference to the notion, apparently fairly widespread, that if salvation was given by grace through faith alone, apart
from works of the law, then Christian behavior and obedience to the
law of God were no longer needed at all. Christians could freely sin
all they wanted, for God would freely forgive them. Many people,
upon hearing that Luther espoused evangelical liberty, and without
bothering to learn what that meant, seemed to think he meant
libertinism. Luther's Roman Catholic opponents claimed that his doctrine of justification by faith alone would lead precisely to this result.
Luther and all the other Protestant reformers consistently denied that
they taught that the gospel allowed anyone to sin freely. John Calvin
was especially forceful on this point, referring to such a false notion
as "carnal security.")

With the catechism completed, Luther's comment from one of his
catechetical sermons, preached on Sept. 14, 1528, took on a truly
public character: "This can be called a children's sermon, or a Bible
of the laity, which is useful for the common people." [6] Some years
later, following a severe illness from which he almost died, he received a request that his works be collected and edited for safe-
keeping and for more widespread distribution. In a letter of July
9, 1537 Luther wrote to Wolfgang Capito in Strassburg, "Regarding
(the plan) to collect my writings in volumes, I am quite cool and not
at all eager about it because, roused by a Saturnian hunger, I would
rather see them all devoured. For I acknowledge none of them to be

[5] Theodore G. Tappert, ed., *The Book of Concord: The Confessions of
the Evangelical Lutheran Church* (Philadelphia: Fortress, 1959), p. 338.

[6] Translated by the editor from *D. Martin Luthers Werke: Kritische
Gesamtausgabe,* vol. 30, part I (Weimar: Hermann Böhlaus Nachfolger,
1910), p. 27.

really a book of mine, except perhaps the one *On the Bound Will* (*De Servo Arbitrio,* published in 1525 as a response to Erasmus' book *De Libero Arbitrio, On the Free Will*) and the Catechism." [7] Luther felt these were the only two books out of all his immense literary production that deserved to be remembered and preserved. In light of the universal admiration given to his *Small Catechism,* he could well be pleased with it. His own evaluation of it meant the most to him, however.

[7] *LW,* vol. 50, pp. 172-73.

II

THE SIGNIFICANCE
OF THE CATECHISMS
FOR CHRISTIAN FAITH
AND THE CHRISTIAN CHURCH

The spread of Luther's reforming ideas across Europe in the 1520s created a lively market for all of his writings. When his catechisms appeared, ideally suited as they were for the needs of the churches and of families, they were widely distributed. At least two translations were made into Latin almost immediately. As the international language of the 16th century, Latin made writings available to the educated classes of all nations of Europe. The first of these editions had an important influence on Scandinavian church life. The second was widely used in central Europe and Germany in particular and was reprinted repeatedly as late as the 18th century. One of these editions reached England very early, and had a great impact on the students at Cambridge and Oxford universities. As a result the Roman Catholic authorities felt compelled to place the Small and Large catechisms, together with about 20 other works of Luther, on their *Index of Prohibited Books* in 1529—the first year of the catechisms' existence. Luther's two catechisms were quickly giving him an international reputation. More importantly, they were contributing to an international revival of Christian religious life at all levels of society, from the peasant farm in Germany to the educated classes at the top levels of English society.

Probably as a result of this early scholarly interest in Luther's work, the *Small Catechism* was also translated into Greek and Hebrew, the ancient biblical languages, so that appropriate comparisons could be made with the original biblical texts. Seldom has a book prepared for the religious training of children and for the devotional life of common people attracted such attention from the learned!

Other translations were also being made which were to have a more direct influence on large numbers of people. In Germany, the *Small Catechism* was published in several regional dialects. For several of these tongues, it was the first literary document. The same was true for some sections of Poland, the Baltic countries, and Hungary. By the end of the 1530s, virtually every European language in common use became a vehicle for this remarkable handbook. Religiously, it was instrumental in winning large numbers of Europeans to a Lutheran understanding of Christian faith and worship. Wherever Lutheran churches developed, the catechism played a large part. In those areas where the catechism introduced people to a literature of their own and helped them establish a national education program based on religious nurture, the impact of the book has been incalculable.

During the latter part of the 16th century the *Small Catechism* (which quickly overshadowed the *Large Catechism* in public significance) became an institution in German religious and educational life. For example, in Saxony, Luther's home territory, the *Church Order* made specific provision for the use of the *Small Catechism* regularly in worship, in religious instruction, and in home devotional use. It became the heart of the *kinderlehre* (literally, "the children's teaching," the equivalent of modern Sunday school or confirmation classes). At Wittenberg after 1533, four two-week series of sermons on the catechism were preached every year. In many other parishes similar patterns were established. The excellence of the catechism, recognized by authorities in church and state, made possible its wholesale application in nurturing the people of Saxony in the gospel.

Unfortunately, the very support which gave the *Small Catechism* such broad recognition also became a hindrance to the most effective educational use of this valuable tool. It was not long before governmental approval of the catechism evolved into governmental control over its use. The catechism became a weapon in the hands of church and state authorities to enforce loyalty to Lutheranism and obedience to the regulations of the Lutheran state clergy. Attendance at catechetical sermons was required. Failure to know the catechism—that is, not being able to *recite* it—was sufficient reason in some areas and towns for keeping people away from Holy Communion, and in some places such ignorance was enough to deny marriage in the church. Such practices created an oppressive atmosphere which made "learning the catechism" a burden rather than an opportunity.

While we now recognize how inappropriate such methods and such attitudes are, and would be quick to spurn such practices, we can perhaps understand them better when we recall the hostile environment in which the 16th century Reformation was carried out. Luther and the other reformers lashed out strongly against what they felt was a distortion of the Christian gospel by the medieval church. The Roman Catholic church, in turn, brought the full weight of its authority to bear against its critics. The atmosphere was charged with a combative spirit, and lines were harshly drawn between competing loyalties. Acceptance of Luther's catechism was the one means open to the common people to express their opinion. Thus one's attitude toward this little book involved more than just educational methods. The people were choosing sides. The few voices raised in favor of toleration or a more moderate view were quickly overwhelmed. In such an atmosphere everyone became defensive. Wherever any religious group or church dominated, it demanded compliance with its views and its practices. All others were to be excluded.

Such attitudes became so commonplace that after Luther's death even his own followers became divided about who represented his views most faithfully. For approximately 30 years the in-house debates between Lutheran theologians over the nature of the gospel went on. The most divisive issues were settled in the *Formula of Concord* of 1577. As a result, Lutheranism found a new clarity about the gospel and discovered the relief of reconciliation. The *Book of Concord* of 1580 was published to bring together in one volume the six confessional documents of Lutheranism. Both the *Small Catechism* and the *Large Catechism* were included in the collection to symbolize and actualize the importance of clear teaching about the fundamental features of the Christian faith. These works were also familiar to most Lutheran people.

Although the *Formula of Concord* restored peace within the Lutheran camp, it did not encourage the development of improved methods of teaching the catechisms. The educational patterns set in the years of struggle and controversy were so firmly entrenched by this time that no real effort was made to improve them. The pastors and teachers were better informed about the content of the faith, but their approach to children militated against the love which the gospel proclaimed. Luther's text was learned primarily by memorization rather than by understanding. Children were required to get the words right. They had little opportunity to enter into the learning process. The catechisms' questions were treated more as a challenge to take a stand than as an opportunity to communicate understanding about the message of God's mercy in Christ. Many pastors, trained as university theologians, regarded the teaching of children as beneath their dignity. They assigned the task to lay teachers more concerned to satisfy their pastoral superiors than to help their pupils discover the gospel in the catechism. There were exceptions to this, of course, but the practice was common. Such instruction became a mechanical church ritual, remote from the real life of the people.

The exceptions to this general situation were notable simply because they were exceptions. Johann Arndt's fine book, *True Christianity* (first published in 1609) became a Protestant devotional classic, running through many German editions and translated into the languages of every European country with a sizeable Lutheran population. Many immigrants brought copies of it to the United States as much as two centuries later. Arndt captured the evangelical style that the words of Luther's catechism embraced, but which training in church and school had obscured. Johann Gerhard was another notable exception, and there were some others. However, the overall situation was not appreciably changed until a new movement arose within Protestantism, and especially within Lutheranism, to give a new impetus to more effective communication of the message of the gospel. That movement has been called *Pietism*.

Philip Jacob Spener was the prime mover within German pietism. While serving as a Lutheran pastor at Frankfurt, he became interested in changing the character and improving the quality of catechetical instruction. He was willing to teach children himself, and he urged them to study the Bible along with the catechism. He often asked them to express the meanings of Luther's explanations in their own words. He also promoted the private, personal use of the catechism as a devotional aid. In short, he advocated much of what Luther had hoped might happen with his little book. Through such means, and especially through his personal interest and involvement, he used his considerable influence to encourage others to work for more effective use of the catechism. August Hermann Francke gave further impetus to this effort by training and sending out teachers from the various institutions he directed at Halle to parishes throughout Germany and around the world. The Pietist movement had its own history in each country. In Scandinavian lands, it stimulated many teachers to produce their own explanations of the catechism that incorporated their views. Particularly influential among Scandinavian Lutherans, both in Europe and America, was the 1737 work of Bishop Erik Pontoppidan of Denmark, *Truth to Piety* (*Sandhed til Gudfrygtighed*).

On the heels of the new impulses given to vital religion by Pietism, a new intellectual movement in German universities called *Rationalism* focused attention on education in ways that were to affect catechetical instruction. Although Rationalism created serious problems for theologians, primarily in the view that religion could be grasped in a definitive way by human reason, educators found valuable tools for more effective teaching in the insights of rationalist thinkers. These scholars emphasized that memorization was ineffective without prior understanding, and so they encouraged such memorization only after students were helped to understand the material they were studying. Perhaps the most far-reaching of their insights was the insistence that teachers adapt their instruction to the intellectual development of their students. As a corollary to this, they urged that students become active participants in the learning process, cooperating partners with the teacher. New catechetical textbooks appeared discussing the art of questioning, beginning with what was familiar to the student. Suddenly children in "catechism classes" had an opportunity to learn and think for themselves—a situation bright with hope for education and for a new theological seriousness and power, but risky for theological orthodoxy.

Helpful as these new methods were, Rationalism finally proved to be too intellectually barren to be a revitalizing factor for religious life in Europe. After an interval of some years, a more distinctly religious movement appeared in Germany in the 1830s, bringing with it new resources for revitalizing faith in a church setting. This "church revival" drew people to the Bible and the church's tradition in order to foster faith and Christian living. It also sparked a new interest in catechesis (catechetical instruction), in Luther's *Small Catechism*, and in the introduction of new explanations for it. One of the most distinguished of 19th century historians, Leopold von Ranke, wrote in 1839, "The Catechism, which he (Luther) published in the year 1529—of which he said, that he repeated it himself with devotion, old doctor as he was—is as childlike as it is profound, as intelligible as simple and sublime. Happy the man whose soul has been nourished with it, and who holds fast to it! It contains enduring comfort in every affliction, and under a slight husk, the kernel of truths able to satisfy the wisest of the wise." [8] Wilhelm Loehe, who exercised a lasting influence on German-American Lutheranism, also wrote an explanation for the catechism during this same period.

An additional feature of this churchly movement was the particular attention it gave to the study of biblical history as part of catechesis. This study revived Luther's claim that the catechism was biblical in origin and a faithful summation of the basic content of the Bible. Spener had repeated this assertion, and this later movement reaffirmed the conviction that no true appreciation of the catechism is possible without its being closely associated with the Bible. Without a doubt, when teachers have made a direct connection between the teachings of the Bible and those of the catechism, the latter has been a more effective aid for promoting and sustaining Christian faith.

On the American scene, the earliest Lutheran arrivals accompanied the Dutch settlers who came to New Amsterdam (now New York City) in 1623 and the years following. The earliest Swedish Lutheran colonists came to Delaware in 1638. In both settlements, Luther's *Small Catechism* was the primary textbook for religious instruction among the Lutheran children. One interesting feature of this period

[8] Leopold von Ranke, *History of the Reformation in Germany*, vol. 2, Robert A. Johnson, ed., Sarah Austin, trans. (New York: Frederick Ungar Publishing Co., 1966 [reprint of 1905 edition]), p. 466.

was the translation of the *Small Catechism* into the language of the Delaware tribe. This was the first literary document in one of the native American languages. It antedated John Eliot's translation of the Bible into the language of the native Americans of Massachusetts, long thought to be the first such translation, by about 16 years. Thus on this continent, as in Europe during the period of the Reformation and in later years, the *Small Catechism* was used for the work of missions and for evangelical outreach as well as for the nurture of children baptized in the Christian faith.

In the next century, the work of Henry Melchior Muhlenberg in Pennsylvania, New York, and other states laid substantial foundations for the establishment of Lutheranism in America. Although German immigrants brought catechisms with them, the supply was far from adequate for the needs of the many new congregations being organized. In 1749, Peter Brunnholz edited the catechism that was, with some later editing, used in the Ministerium of Pennsylvania for more than a century. The first printing of this text was done by J. Boehm and one Benjamin Franklin in Philadelphia. Germans in Europe also continued to provide their own editions for the congregations in the New World.

The vast wave of immigration from Northern Europe which began in the first half of the 19th century and swelled rapidly after the Civil War, lasting until just about World War I, brought a new influx of religious vitality to the young and spreading Lutheran communities. It also brought a corresponding mixture of translations of the Bible and the catechism. The transition from the European languages to English in the newly adopted American homeland obligated the immigrants to speed up the process of translating the documents of their faith into the new tongue for the sake of their children. The first English *Small Catechism* to be produced in the United States appeared in 1795. Many other editions and translations were to follow. The story of that process is too long and involved for detailed treatment in this essay.

The situation, however, might well be portrayed in the account of the early Norwegian preacher named Elling Eielsen. After his arrival in this country, he worked primarily in the Fox River settlements in Illinois. When the Norwegian settlers recognized they would need English-language catechisms for their children, who were quickly learning the new language, Eielsen *walked* from Illinois to New York City in 1841 to purchase the necessary English texts for his people. Such zeal for the cause of Christian education was not customary, even among hardy pioneer settlers; but it was a reflection of a widely felt need for education if the second generation of immigrant families were to survive in the new land. That the catechism was the book selected for this purpose indicates the high esteem in which it was held, even far away from the homeland of the Reformation.

In the second half of the 19th century, the numbers of Europeans coming to the United States reached its peak. Among them were those who had experienced the religious awakenings and revivals of Europe. The newcomers also brought new supplies of Bibles, hymnals, and catechisms. The settlement process was repeated on a larger scale than a half-century earlier, and again the catechism played no small part in undergirding the work of the pastors and lay leaders who planted the old faith in the new world. By 1929, no American Lutheran church body was without an English translation of Luther's *Small Catechism*. By then, the wave of immigration had ebbed, but the work of Christian nurture went on. The churches of the present are still benefiting from the labors of faithful forebears, who understood that Christian education was vital for the continuity of the church. For all those early Lutherans, the catechism was the key to this continuity.

The counterpart of the story of the *Small Catechism* in the United States could be told in many other nations around the world as well. Such a story is far beyond the scope of this overview, but it should be said that just as in the 16th century the *Small Catechism* found its way all across Europe, so now it can be found wherever there are Lutherans anywhere in the world. Wherever Lutheran missionaries or evangelists have traveled and worked they have brought the catechism with them and have used it effectively to acquaint people with the Lutheran faith and help them pass it on. The valuable work of translation performed by missionaries over the past 150 years in Asia, Africa, Central and South America, and the scattered islands of all the oceans has often meant the creation of literary languages out of the spoken dialects of those lands. The Bible has been the primary instrument for this work, but in some instances the *Small Catechism* has also proven valuable for this purpose. As a general rule, wherever Lutheran mission work has been carried on, there Luther's catechism has played a significant part in the evangelization of the people and the education of their children, lay leaders, and pastors.

As the 19th century progressed, vast changes were coming over the western world. Traditional ways of thinking about the world and of viewing life itself were giving way to new ideas—fostered by the rapid growth of the physical, psychological, and social sciences and the rapid expansion of technology and industry. Accompanying these changes was a secular shift in mood. People began to view life, the fulfillment of life, and expectations for human happiness only in terms of the visible, measurable world. To many, the new discoveries meant that God, or any spiritual dimension, was no longer necessary to explain life. Knowledge of physical and human nature was thought to be capable of supplying answers to all human questions and of providing resources to meet all human needs.

One accomplishment of this mood change was the effort made to remove all religious education from the public school curriculum. This was especially true in European countries where religious education was conducted under government auspices. Catechetical instruction was regarded by the exponents of the new view as a form of indoctrination which was no longer desirable. The separation of church and state was widely regarded as the only appropriate basis for the organization of religious education.

Religious liberalism, so prominent in Europe between 1860 and 1920, came later to the Western Hemisphere. Some theologians and educators in the United States espoused these views prior to World War I, but they made much more of an impact here in the 1920s. The significant liberal-fundamentalist debates within American Protestantism during that decade, while not involving Lutheran churches directly nor Lutheran individuals in significant numbers, nevertheless had their impact on the religious environment in which American Lutheranism began to mature before and after World War II. The relative isolation of American Lutheran church bodies from such encounters meant that traditional patterns of religious instruction were maintained intact at a time when similar programs in other denominational families were struggling. During that period, the *Small Catechism* continued to be the primary resource for confirmation instruction in all the major Lutheran bodies in this country.

In the years following World War II, most church bodies made substantial investments in the creation of new religious education materials. New textbooks appeared, and new programs for the preparation of volunteer church school teachers were initiated. Modern communications made the dissemination of these materials possible even to the most isolated congregations. New educational methods were developed related to similar advances in public education. Sometimes the catechisms had a place in the new programs, and sometimes they did not.

A key factor in this process was a marked shift toward student-centered instruction. Impressions students received from their own experiences and life situations became the starting point for religious learning. Christianity was taught as a message that related to real life, and the whole of life. All of this was occurring during a time when there were powerful demands for social change in public life.

Then in the 1970s a certain reaction set in. Many teachers and parents using the new curricula began to complain that they missed the familiar Bible stories and lessons. Others missed the familiar words of Luther's catechism. Church people who had struggled painfully during the 1960s with questions related to the war in Vietnam, racism, and world hunger, now turned to inwardness and to personal growth in spirituality. As the mood changed, a widespread nostalgia recalled a simpler, often romanticized past and undergirded a more private approach to religion.

In this setting, we have reached the 450th anniversary of the publication of Luther's two catechisms. Like all such anniversaries, it provides us an opportunity to rediscover the wealth of religious insight these books have for us. Certainly we can all benefit from a new familiarity with Luther's clarity about the gospel. But we have to make some choices.

How are we to use these resources in ways that do justice both to the texts and to our best understanding of the ways students learn? Further, will this celebration only serve to glorify the past, or will it become the occasion for affirming the lasting values of our religious heritage for our generation and for the real needs of tomorrow's church? Luther once moved his church into a new future. He can help us to do the same for the church of our time—if we will keep intact the integrity of both his words and our own real needs.

III

SOME SUGGESTIONS
FOR TEACHING
LUTHER'S CATECHISMS

How can the catechisms of Luther function for us today? Can we find ways to use them in the religious nurture of our children and congregations that will be helpful for us and for the church in the 20th century? In this section, some proposals are advanced to stimulate the thinking and imagination of parents, church school teachers, and pastors so that they can make the best possible use of the resources for Christian faith and living given to us in these time-tested texts.

New Possibilities for Asking Questions

The most effective teaching begins by giving attention to the student or learner. It continues by keeping the focus on the student throughout the teaching process. This does not mean that every teacher needs to be a specialist in developmental psychology, however. It does mean that whoever teaches must be interested in students as individual persons, sensitive to their readiness for the learning situation at hand, alert to special needs or problems individual students may have, and *willing* to attempt to meet students at their own level of understanding. These are not so much skills as attitudes. They reflect a teacher's openness to meet students where they are. Children are especially sensitive to teacher attitudes. They recognize who is trying to go *with* them into learning and who is trying to teach *at* them. When they realize their teacher is "on their side," they are more willing to join the teacher in the learning process.

The question-and-answer technique employed by Luther, as well as by many other writers of catechisms, creates an immediate problem in this regard. Luther, of course, had the task of producing the answers to the question, What does this mean? The burden was on him as a teacher to come up with the answers in such a style that children, on hearing them, would be helped to understand. By our day, however, the catechization tradition within Lutheranism has reversed the roles. Until recently, it was common for the teacher to ask a question, and students had the responsibility to give the answer. Not only that, but

often students had to give just exactly the "correct" (printed) answer
and nothing else. It is easy to see why children felt more obligated
to give the correctly *worded* answer than to seek understanding
about what was being asked.

That pattern is not the only way to use questions, however. As we
have seen, in supplying the answers in his catechisms Luther *acted
out* the proper role of the teacher. One reformer, Urbanus Rhegius
(see p. 17 above) suggested the same role when he recommended
in his catechism of 1523 that students ask the questions and teachers
provide the answers. (See Exod. 12:26-27 and Josh. 4:6-7 for Old
Testament examples of children asking and their elders answering
the significant questions of faith.) It is most appropriate for teachers,
once a commandment, article of the Creed, or petition of the Lord's
Prayer has been presented, to invite questions about it from the students. If a student raises a question that a teacher feels unable to
answer, it need not pose a threat. Quite the opposite. This is that
much-sought-after opportunity for teacher and students to learn together as they search for the answer—together. Such occasions are
often the times when we learn the most and the best.

If catechetical instruction is to become student-centered, then
teachers (including parents and pastors) will have to work at encouraging students to raise their own questions about the materials
being studied. Many people fear that asking a question will be interpreted as a sign of either ignorance or brashness. We who teach
too often create that environment, and we need to turn that ex-
pectation around so that students can feel free to ask what they want
to ask. The catechisms provide the raw material for many questions
and for lively discussion. Children, who are curious by nature, will
feel free to ask their questions if we create an atmosphere that is
open.

Many will notice that the most recent text of the *Small Catechism*
states the question differently than in the past. It once read, "What
does this mean?" Now the question reads, "What does this mean *for
us?*" This latter form reflects the importance Luther attaches to
the words "for you" in his last question about the Lord's Supper in
the *Small Catechism*. Luther's own religious experience of God's grace
assured him that God's mercy had been given in Christ *for him*. (See
Luther's extended comment on the phrase "for me" in his commentary
on Gal. 2:20 in vol. 26 of the American Edition of *Luther's Works*,
pp. 176-79.) This modification of the text, slight as it may appear,
makes a notable difference in our use of the question. It gives each
one who hears the question the right to *discover his or her own meanings* in the text. It opens the door to further student-centered learning.
We should let students have the freedom and delight of discovering

what the ancient biblical message says to them *without having to be concerned whether or not that is what the teacher wants them to learn.* Only when teachers are this open will students make the lessons of the Bible and the catechism their own.

Both of Luther's catechisms provide a tantalizing "grab-bag" of religious gems to which students of all ages ought to have free and ready access. The teacher who can arouse their curiosity to the point where they are free to pull out an item or two and ask, "What's this?" and "What is that all about?" and "What has that got to do with me?" will find zest and excitement in this teaching.

Some Comments on Methods

Luther insisted that the content of the catechisms was drawn out of the Bible, and that it summarized some of the essential teachings of the Bible. It is still important to relate the catechisms to the Bible so that students can realize the vital connection between them.

Four of the five chief parts of the catechism—the Commandments, the Lord's Prayer, and the sacraments of Baptism and the Lord's Supper—are drawn directly from the Bible. Luther's explanations of each of these parts are derived from his study and reflection on what the Bible says about these topics. The fifth part, the Apostles' Creed, is a summary of the church's faith in the triune God revealed in the Scriptures. Children and adults need to have these connections made explicit, so that all who study the catechisms will know that their religious heritage is biblically based and remains true to scriptural teaching.

This important linkage suggests that Bible study ought to be a regular accompaniment to catechism study. Such study ought not to be limited only to those passages of the Bible which bear directly on the part of the catechism under study, however. Students deserve the opportunity to make at least a preliminary acquaintance with the main themes of the biblical story, the central thrust of the history of the people of Israel and the life of Jesus, and the basic faith decisions about God, self, neighbor, and world which the biblical writers affirm. In addition, the Bible and the catechisms supplement each other uniquely. Biblical narratives abound with illustrations of God's activity in creation, redemption, and sanctification. Others show the role of prayer in a believer's life. Still others portray the gripping human-divine drama of sin, forgiveness, and reconciliation. Likewise, the catechism provides some excellent summaries of what the Bible teaches. After dealing with a particular biblical segment, students will learn that Luther's knack for going to the heart of the Bible marks him as an especially gifted Christian teacher.

This leads into a second observation on method. Both of the catechisms, but the *Small Catechism* in particular, contain many unusually apt expressions about the Christian faith. Many of these are well worth remembering word-for-word. This is not to suggest that we return to a pattern of rote memorization of the parts of the catechism. We have discovered how unprofitable in the long run such a procedure is. However, when a student or teacher finds some line or phrase that strikes them as meaningful or especially insightful, then the time is ripe for suggesting that the segment be repeated aloud, and then repeated again, and woven into subsequent conversations, until it does become memorized. Pastors who use some of the key passages from the catechisms from time to time will find that Lutherans will once again come to appreciate Luther's gift for expressing the deep things of the Christian faith in moving words.

Third, four of the five parts of the catechism—the Creed, the Lord's Prayer, and the two sacraments of Baptism and the Lord's Supper—appear in the liturgies of Lutheran churches. Children or adults who begin to study the catechism after having participated in the worship life of a congregation will recognize these parts as familiar friends. Meaningful worship should prepare us well to study the catechism. Likewise, catechism study should enable us to worship with new insight and appreciation. The opportunity for this interplay is available to all Lutheran congregations, but the most effective combination will occur when teachers and worship leaders plan and work together to take optimum advantage of these built-in opportunities.

Catechism teachers (catechists), by taking time to help students appreciate what is happening in liturgical actions and understand what they mean, will find students more ready to participate in such actions. In some settings—confirmation classes, high school classes, youth group meetings—young people will welcome opportunities to develop their own liturgies on the basis of what they have learned from the catechism as well as from their life experiences. A sensitive guide at such a time will not only encourage students' creative talents but will also help them develop a new appreciation for the worship of the whole congregation. Although the Ten Commandments are not specifically found in Lutheran liturgies, they could serve admirably for a service involving the confession of sin. In the 1531 edition of the *Small Catechism* Luther included a section on confession between Baptism and the Lord's Supper. There he suggested the use of the Commandments for self-examination of believers in preparation for Holy Communion. This practice, adapted for our own situation, might well be of interest again in our churches.

Fourth, we have all experienced how effectively a lesson can be communicated by telling a story. Storytelling has been the primary teaching device for the human race as far back as we can trace our history. Everyone delights in a good story, whether old or new. Since the catechisms are not written in this style, catechists will find that stories which illustrate catechism lessons will enhance the interest students show in learning. Such stories, of course, serve best when they arise out of recognizable life situations familiar to the students. One word of caution is in order, however. Stories must ring true to life, whether they recount historical incidents or not. A story that does not communicate authenticity "turns off" students and can develop skepticism about what they are being taught. If we can avoid this trap, the stories we tell can be an effective means for passing on our heritage. Experienced teachers will also recognize the value of role plays and other forms of dramatic storytelling in which students can "live into" the stories and reenact their lessons.

One additional suggestion is offered which grows out of the sections dealing with the sacraments, although it has much broader applicability. The physical elements used by our Lord in the two sacraments teach us that God comes to us through the common things of our everyday life. Bread and water are common to all humanity. At times Luther suggested that God *never* comes to us *except* through what is concrete in human experience—people, material things, historical events. Luther was suspicious, and even critical, of any revelation that came by "spiritual" means only. The best revelation God gave us of himself was the fully human person, Jesus of Nazareth. That this human being was, at the same time, the true son of God, lies at the very heart of the Christian faith. This is incarnation, coming "in the flesh" (Latin: *in carne*). The principle of incarnation operates elsewhere, too. The Bible comes to us on paper and written in ink, using human language to record God's gracious dealings with Israel and all the world. The sacraments communicate the benefits of that grace through elements that are familiar to us all in our common daily life.

This tells us that any object, person, or event can provide an occasion and opportunity for learning. A rock, a piece of driftwood, a bird's feather, a crippled child in a wheelchair, a tornado, a birth— these only hint at the infinite variety of teaching aids we are all surrounded with wherever we live and teach. Nor need a teacher feel compelled to assemble such resources all alone. Children will bring, or will have, their own wares with them. Usually they are more ready than not to share their possessions as means of throwing new light on ancient truth.

These suggestions about method grow out of experience with the catechisms themselves. Conscientious teachers are aware of much more that could be described than can be dealt with here. They also recognize that they have to pick and choose among many creative possibilities to find what is best-suited to their own teaching styles and personalities. Luther himself used his imagination in teaching the catechisms, as we learn from his own report: "The Commandments are sung in two versions, [9] as well as painted, printed, carved, and recited by the children morning, noon, and night. I know of no manner in which we do not use them, unless it be that we unfortunately do not practice and paint them with our deeds and our life as we should." [10]

Whatever approach to learning we use, let it serve to help our students hear for themselves the message of God which has been passed on to our generation through the catechisms. Let every method and every means serve the students' needs.

Settings in which to Use the Catechisms

Up to this point we have assumed a classroom (confirmation class, Sunday church school class, adult class) as the place where the catechisms can best be used. Very likely this setting will continue to provide the best opportunity for regular catechism instruction. In fact, there may be additional grade levels at which the catechisms could be used where we have been hesitant to do so, especially at adult levels. Congregations would be well served by checking the possibilities.

Luther, however, never intended the catechisms only for classroom use. The German subtitles Luther placed under the heading of each of the five chief parts of the *Small Catechism* read, in English, "In the plain form in which the head of the family shall teach them to his household." Thus for Luther the home where the family gathered was the key place for hearing and learning about the catechism. Luther expected parents to take responsibility for the Christian nurture of their own children. At home, the imagination and ingenuity of parents —and children!—should have full rein to proceed in whatever way seems most helpful. Parents can begin to read to their children from the catechism at home. Prayers, using the words and phrases of the catechisms, can be taught and used. Children can be encouraged to begin composing their own prayers using some of the same expressions. The time together around the table gives a good opportunity for a child to ask the questions about what all these things mean within that family. With such questions, the doors open to a family conversation about the heart of their faith. Such conversations are not automatic. Sensitive parents will have to be alert to the opportunities

[9] Luther wrote two hymns based on the Commandments. See *LW*, vol. 53, pp. 278-79, 281.
[10] From "Against the Antinomians," *LW*, vol. 47, p. 109.

as they arise, and reinforce the learnings that develop with Bible stories or perhaps a hymn or a story of their own. If we are alert to Luther's suggestion, our homes can again become a fountain of religious life among our people.

As we have seen, the liturgical celebrations of a congregation provide a variety of occasions for the use of the catechisms. The Apostles' Creed and the Lord's Prayer are incorporated into almost every Sunday morning worship service. In addition, baptisms occur with some frequency, and Holy Communion is usually celebrated on a regular schedule. By incorporating some elements of Luther's explanations into these services in a way that does not interrupt the flow of worship, a congregation could lift the appreciation of all worshipers for what they are saying and doing each week. Some congregations occasionally substitute one of Luther's explanations to an article of the Creed for the use of the full Creed itself. Parts of a litany using catechism selections could be developed rather easily. Given the sermonic origins of the catechisms, pastors might well use their sermons for reiterating or emphasizing what the catechisms have to say about a specific theme or text. When listeners are reminded about what is familiar to them, they listen more attentively and grasp more easily the significance of what they are hearing.

Within the wider circle of activities of a congregation, there are a number of chances for focusing on the catechism in new ways. Meetings of church councils or other official boards and committees often open with some form of devotion or meditation. In some church councils, specific times for study and reflection are made a regular part of each meeting's agenda. These times are tailor-made for stimulating adult interest in the religious and theological heritage of the congregation, matters about which lay church leaders should be informed. Many are already asking for something like this. Other special groups (youth, women, study groups, action committees, and others) provide their own opportunities for placing the catechism in fresh contexts, where it can speak to people in the midst of their present situation.

Finally, the personal character of the *Small Catechism* suggests that individuals might well find it helpful in personal devotional activity or in times of special meditation and reflection, as Luther often did. Individualized study, whether directed by a teacher or not, could well use the catechisms as background sources for exploring the theological terrain of our own times. Lay people with questions on their minds will find the catechisms useful guides as they grapple with the complex concerns of 20th century life.

The Ten Commandments, after all, provide basic ethical affirmations from which Christians can draw substantial guidance in grappling with such current ethical questions as abortion, the preservation of family life, sexual morality, modern genetic research, human rights and human justice, economic and political systems, world hunger, the rule of law and the like, to say nothing about the unforeseen questions the next generation is likely to raise. The Commandments do not promise simple answers to every question, but they do give us perspectives for considering our problems which need to be reaffirmed today.

In the face of cultism and occultism, the Creed makes affirmations about God and our relationship with God that are invaluable for people of all ages. The catechisms' insights into the meaning of the sacraments, with their strong emphasis on the grace of God, can recover for us all a new appreciation of that grace. The Lord's Prayer can open new vistas on the possibilities for rich new forms and meanings in spirituality. In the midst of all this, not only pastors and other professional theologians but also all Christians can benefit from thoughtful reflection about how our catechisms can help us live more confidently as Christians in our own time.

Some Final Comments

What follow are three topics that do not fall neatly into a broad category. The first is the question about the difference between the Small and Large catechisms. Does the difference in size, in amount of material presented, mean anything? The longer format of the *Large Catechism* enabled Luther to use his sermons more directly in developing this text. He had room for illustrations, he could refer to the discussions and disputes he was involved in as a reformer, and could illuminate some of the discussion questions in this way. In the longer text, the reader senses the impact of Luther's feelings and actions through his language. The context of his times begins to emerge from the background. The points of controversy on certain questions, and the reasons for Luther's positions on those questions, are clarified in ways not possible in the *Small Catechism*. The expanded explanations of the *Large Catechism* provide a broader treatment of each part that is especially valuable for all who teach or study these works.

Second, both catechisms are received by Lutheran churches around the world as official confessional documents, defining what Lutheranism is for all these churches. In the 16th century there was an urgent need for churches to establish their identity as Lutherans. Since the *Small Catechism* was the most widely known and used document of this kind, it was clear that it was already functioning as the identifying symbol for most Lutherans. Few had read or heard about any of the others. Thus the *Small Catechism* was a "natural" for this role. The *Large Catechism* took on the same character simply because it was readily identified with the *Small Catechism*.

Over the years, some have argued that using the catechisms as confessional documents in this way has diminished their effectiveness as teaching instruments. It cannot be denied that using the catechisms as a text for orthodoxy led to a certain rigidity in teaching them. However, the possibilities for a more flexible approach to catechetical instruction are considerable, given the character and composition of these texts. At a time when Lutherans are asking one another what it means to affirm these four-centuries-old confessional writings, it may well be that the simplicity of the catechisms can help us achieve a realistic understanding both of the human quality of confessional statements and of their true value as means for witnessing to the faith we hold. At the same time, an openness to capitalize on the teaching values they contain will help us appreciate what they can do for us. Once we see the catechisms as means to an end, rather than as ends in themselves, these fine books will once again be valued among us.

Finally, something remains to be said about the order of the chief parts of the *Small Catechism*. We have already noted (see p. 16 above) that once Luther established the order we now recognize, he did not depart from it. However, there were others, including Lutherans, who preferred a different arrangement. For example, as early as 1527 and 1528 Johann Agricola, who had once been one of Luther's colleagues on the faculty at Wittenberg, published catechisms of his own in which he followed the order previously used by the Hussite catechisms of the Bohemian Brethren in Czechoslovakia. In this order, Baptism came first, in order to teach about the means of entry into the Christian community. It was Agricola's understanding that the gospel came before the law—that the preaching of forgiveness should precede preaching about repentance—and thus the teaching about Baptism and the Creed should come before the Commandments. In this order, the Commandments are to show forgiven Christians the pattern life should follow as it is lived by faith. Later Lutherans were to refer to this as "the third use of the law." This understanding of the function of the law was similar to that of the medieval church, which customarily placed the Creed first in its catechisms. In this way the Creed served as the past foundation for a present emphasis on repentance, or rather on the Sacrament of Penance.

Both in Agricola's plan and in the older medieval orders, Luther felt that the work of God in redemption and in Baptism was relegated too much to the past. Both patterns led to the conclusion that the present concern for the Christian lay primarily in living up to the

Commandments for the development of one's Christian life. According to Luther, there were two problems with this view. In the first place, it did not take sin seriously enough. It assumed too much about the capacity of the Christian to fulfill the Commandments. In the second place, the view concentrated the Christian's energies on his or her own efforts to be a Christian before God. This, to Luther, lay dangerously close to the gross pattern of "works righteousness" against which he had fought so strongly in the opening years of his reforming work. Luther was convinced that while these other patterns gave first place to Baptism and the Creed, and seemed thereby to accord primary honor to God's work, in actual fact they functioned to put Baptism and God's work into the past and to make Christian behavior the prime consideration, rather than the grace of God.

After considering these other arrangements, Luther concluded that his first insight was correct. The Commandments should come first, he felt, because—when properly taught—they show us our sinfulness and need of the Savior. This, he was convinced, was the first function of God's law—its primary use. The Commandments were intended to remind everyone, including Christians, that we are in daily need of God's forgiveness and grace. Baptism is not a thing of the past only, for it symbolizes a daily dying to sin and a daily renewal of life through faith in Christ (see Luther's fourth question on the Sacrament of Baptism in the *Small Catechism*). Luther felt that by beginning with the Commandments, Christians would appreciate anew each day what God had done for them in Baptism and as recounted in the Creed. These aspects of our faith would not then simply be relegated to some time in the past, as ancient history, but would rather become living realities in the present for Christians, leading them to give thanks to God daily for forgiveness and redemption. The primary concern for Christians would thus be God's grace toward sinners, not our human efforts to improve ourselves.

Over the years, not all Lutherans (and not even all Lutheran pastors and teachers) have shared Luther's views on this matter. Much catechism instruction focused primarily on the Commandments as God's regulations for Christian living, and has underemphasized their function as God's mirror, showing us our condition and need of God's mercy. Simply by spending more time on this one section than on the other chief parts of the catechism, students have picked up the notion that the law is more important than the gospel. (A fairly recent major survey of church youth indicated they saw Christianity in that light.[11]) It is ironic that this has resulted in the church

[11] Merton P. Strommen and others, *A Study of Generations: Report of a Two-Year Study of 5,000 Lutherans Between the Ages of 15-65: Their Beliefs, Values, Attitudes, Behavior* (Minneapolis: Augsburg, 1972), pp. 100-151.

that bears the name of Luther, the one who saw as the primary aim of his life's work the recovery of the gospel of God's grace. It seems to this writer that 20th century teachers could study Luther with profit, and that in a fresh examination of his distinction between the law and the gospel we might find fruitful insights for the teaching of the Christian faith in our day, as he did in his.

On the Design of this Book

What follow are the two catechisms of Luther. We have arranged them in such a way that each item in the *Small Catechism*—each Commandment, each article of the Creed, each petition of the Lord's Prayer—is followed by its counterpart from the *Large Catechism*. Teachers will thus have the two explanations together and will be able to draw on the more extensive explanations of the latter to help them teach and interpret the former. If this organization of the material helps us to make more effective use of the *Small Catechism*, and acquaints the churches again with the content of the *Large Catechism*, then the purpose of this venture will have been achieved.

The text of the *Small Catechism* used here is the 1968 edition in contemporary English published by Augsburg Publishing House and Fortress Press for the Lutheran Church in America, the Lutheran Church—Missouri Synod, and the American Lutheran Church. The text of the *Large Catechism* is from *The Book of Concord*, edited by Theodore G. Tappert and published in 1959 by Fortress Press, which has graciously granted permission for its use here. The text of the *Small Catechism* is centered in a narrower column than the text of the *Large Catechism*, which is printed fully across the page. The footnotes to the *Large Catechism* are those supplied by Tappert.

We have not provided a detailed commentary about each item in the catechisms. Over the years a great deal has been published to meet this need, and the libraries of most pastors and of many congregations will have some of these resources available. One of the better of these is the two-volume work by Herbert Girgensohn, *Teaching Luther's Catechism*, translated by John W. Doberstein (Muhlenberg Press, 1959). Two of the more recent contributions in this field are *Free to Be: A Handbook to Luther's Small Catechism*, by James A. Nestingen and Gerhard O. Forde (Augsburg, 1975), and *Faith and Freedom: The Christian Faith According to the Lutheran Confessions* by Charles S. Anderson (Augsburg, 1977). We endorse the use of any of these with this volume. References to other works in the footnotes will suggest additional reading for those who are interested in further background information or commentary on Luther's catechisms.

THE SMALL CATECHISM
AND THE LARGE CATECHISM
OF DR. MARTIN LUTHER

THE SMALL CATECHISM
of Dr. Martin Luther
for Ordinary Pastors and Preachers

[PREFACE]

Grace, mercy, and peace in Jesus Christ, our Lord, from Martin Luther to all faithful, godly pastors and preachers.

The deplorable conditions which I recently encountered when I | was a visitor[2] constrained me to prepare this brief and simple catechism or statement of Christian teaching. Good God, what wretchedness 2 I beheld! The common people, especially those who live in the country, have no knowledge whatever of Christian teaching, and unfortunately many pastors are quite incompetent and unfitted for teaching. Although the people are supposed to be Christian, are baptized, and 3 receive the holy sacrament, they do not know the Lord's Prayer, the Creed, or the Ten Commandments,[3] they live as if they were pigs and irrational beasts, and now that the Gospel has been restored they have mastered the fine art of abusing liberty.

How will you bishops answer for it before Christ that you have 4 so shamefully neglected the people and paid no attention at all to the duties of your office? May you escape punishment for this! You 5 withhold the cup in the Lord's Supper and insist on the observance of human laws, yet you do not take the slightest interest in teaching the people the Lord's Prayer, the Creed, the Ten Commandments, or a single part of the Word of God. Woe to you forever!

I therefore beg of you for God's sake, my beloved brethren who 6 are pastors and preachers, that you take the duties of your office seriously, that you have pity on the people who are entrusted to your care, and that you help me to teach the catechism to the people, especially those who are young. Let those who lack the qualifications to do better at least take this booklet and these forms and read them to the people word for word in this manner:

In the first place, the preacher should take the utmost care to 7

---

[2]Luther made visitations of congregations in Electoral Saxony and Meissen between Oct. 22, 1528, and Jan. 9, 1529.

[3] This is the order in which these materials appeared in late medieval manuals.

avoid changes or variations in the text and wording of the Ten Commandments, the Creed, the Lord's Prayer, the sacraments, etc. On the contrary, he should adopt one form, adhere to it, and use it repeatedly year after year. Young and inexperienced people must be instructed on the basis of a uniform, fixed text and form. They are easily confused if a teacher employs one form now and another form—perhaps with the intention of making improvements—later on. In this way all the time and labor will be lost.

This was well understood by our good fathers, who were   8 accustomed to use the same form in teaching the Lord's Prayer, the Creed, and the Ten Commandments. We, too, should teach these things to the young and unlearned in such a way that we do not alter a single syllable or recite the catechism differently from year to year. Choose the form that pleases you, therefore, and adhere to it hence-forth. When you preach to intelligent and educated people, you are   9 at liberty to exhibit your learning and to discuss these topics from different angles and in such a variety of ways as you may be capable of. But when you are teaching the young, adhere to a fixed and un-changing form and method. Begin by teaching them the Ten   10 Commandments, the Creed, the Lord's Prayer, etc., following the text word for word so that the young may repeat these things after you and retain them in their memory.

If any refuse to receive your instructions, tell them that they   11 deny Christ and are no Christians. They should not be admitted to the sacrament, be accepted as sponsors in Baptism, or be allowed to participate in any Christian privileges.[4] On the contrary, they should be turned over to the pope and his officials,[5] and even to the devil himself. In addition, parents and employers should refuse to   12 furnish them with food and drink and should notify them that the prince is disposed to banish such rude people from his land.

Although we cannot and should not compel anyone to believe,   13 we should nevertheless insist that the people learn to know how to distinguish between right and wrong according to the standards of those among whom they live and make their living.[6] For anyone who desires to reside in a city is bound to know and observe the laws under whose protection he lives, no matter whether he is a believer or, at heart, a scoundrel or knave.

In the second place, after the people have become familiar with   14 the text, teach them what it means. For this purpose, take the explanations in this booklet, or choose any other brief and fixed

---

[4] Cf. Large Catechism, Short Preface, 1-5.

[5] Diocesan judges who decided disciplinary and other cases; now often alled vicar-generals.

[6] Cf. Large Catechism, Short Preface, 2.

explanations which you may prefer, and adhere to them without 15 changing a single syllable, as stated above with reference to the text. Moreover, allow yourself ample time, for it is not necessary to 16 take up all the parts at once. They can be presented one at a time. When the learners have a proper understanding of the First Commandment, proceed to the Second Commandment, and so on. Otherwise they will be so overwhelmed that they will hardly remember anything at all.

In the third place, after you have thus taught this brief 17 catechism, take up a large catechism[7] so that the people may have a richer and fuller understanding. Expound every commandment, petition, and part, pointing out their respective obligations, benefits, dangers, advantages, and disadvantages, as you will find all of this treated at length in the many books written for this purpose. Lay 18 the greatest weight on those commandments or other parts which seem to require special attention among the people where you are. For example, the Seventh Commandment, which treats of stealing, must be emphasized when instructing laborers and shopkeepers, and even farmers and servants, for many of these are guilty of dishonesty and thievery.[8] So, too, the Fourth Commandment must be stressed when instructing children and the common people in order that they may be encouraged to be orderly, faithful, obedient, and peaceful. Always adduce many examples from the Scriptures to show how God punished and blessed.

You should also take pains to urge governing authorities and 19 parents to rule wisely and educate their children. They must be shown that they are obliged to do so, and that they are guilty of damnable sin if they do not do so, for by such neglect they undermine and lay waste both the kingdom of God and the kingdom of the world and are the worst enemies of God and man. Make very plain to 20 them the shocking evils they introduce when they refuse their aid in the training of children to become pastors, preachers, notaries, etc., and tell them that God will inflict awful punishments on them for these sins. It is necessary to preach about such things. The extent to which parents and governing authorities sin in this respect is beyond telling. The devil also has a horrible purpose in mind.

Finally, now that the people are freed from the tyranny of the 21 pope, they are unwilling to receive the sacrament and they treat it with contempt. Here, too, there is need of exhortation, but with this understanding: No one is to be compelled to believe or to receive the sacrament, no law is to be made concerning it, and no time or place

[7] Luther here refers not only to his own Large Catechism but also to other treatments of the traditional parts of the catechism. See the reference to "many books" in the next sentence.

[8] Cf. Large Catechism, Ten Commandments, 225, 226.

should be appointed for it. We should so preach that, of their   22
own accord and without any law, the people will desire the sacrament
and, as it were, compel us pastors to administer it to them. This can
be done by telling them: It is to be feared that anyone who does not
desire to receive the sacrament at least three or four times a year
despises the sacrament and is no Christian, just as he is no Christian
who does not hear and believe the Gospel. Christ did not say, "Omit
this," or "Despise this," but he said, "Do this, as often as you drink it,"
etc.[9] Surely he wishes that this be done and not that it be omitted and
despised. "*Do* this," he said.

He who does not highly esteem the sacrament suggests thereby   23
that he has no sin, no flesh, no devil, no world, no death, no hell. That
is to say, he believes in none of these, although he is deeply immersed
in them and is held captive by the devil. On the other hand, he
suggests that he needs no grace, no life, no paradise, no heaven, no
Christ, no God, nothing good at all. For if he believed that he was
involved in so much that is evil and was in need of so much that is
good, he would not neglect the sacrament in which aid is afforded
against such evil and in which such good is bestowed. It is not
necessary to compel him by any law to receive the sacrament, for he
will hasten to it of his own accord, he will feel constrained to receive it.
he will insist that you administer it to him.

Accordingly you are not to make a law of this, as the pope has   24
done. All you need to do is clearly to set forth the advantage and
disadvantage, the benefit and loss, the blessing and danger connected
with this sacrament. Then the people will come of their own accord
and without compulsion on your part. But if they refuse to come, let
them be, and tell them that those who do not feel and acknowledge
their great need and God's gracious help belong to the devil. If   25
you do not give such admonitions, or if you adopt odious laws on the
subject, it is your own fault if the people treat the sacrament with
contempt. How can they be other than negligent if you fail to do
your duty and remain silent. So it is up to you, dear pastor and
preacher! Our office has become something different from what it   26
was under the pope. It is now a ministry of grace and salvation.
It subjects us to greater burdens and labors, dangers and tempta-   27
tions, with little reward or gratitude from the world. But Christ
himself will be our reward if we labor faithfully. The Father of all
grace grant it! To him be praise and thanks forever, through Christ,
our Lord. Amen.

⁹ I Cor. 11:25.

THE LARGE CATECHISM
of
Dr. Martin Luther

MARTIN LUTHER'S PREFACE[1]

It is not for trivial reasons that we constantly treat the Cate-   1 chism and strongly urge others to do the same. For we see to our sorrow that many pastors and preachers[2] are very negligent in this respect and despise both their office and this teaching itself. Some because of their great and lofty learning, others because of sheer laziness and gluttony, behave in this matter as if they were pastors or preachers for their bellies' sake and had nothing to do but live off the fat of the land all their days, as they used to do under the papacy.

Everything that they are to teach and preach is now available   2 to them in clear and simple form in the many excellent books which are in reality what the old manuals claimed in their titles to be: "Sermons That Preach Themselves," "Sleep Soundly," "Prepared!" and "Treasury." [3] However, they are not so upright and honest as to buy these books, or if they have them, to examine and read them. Such shameful gluttons and servants of their bellies would make better swineherds or dogkeepers than spiritual guides and pastors.

Now that they are free from the useless, bothersome babbling of   3 the Seven Hours,[4] it would be fine if every morning, noon, and evening they would read, instead, at least a page or two from the Catechism, the Prayer Book,[5] the New Testament, or something else from the Bible and would pray the Lord's Prayer for themselves and their parishioners. In this way they might show honor and gratitude to the Gospel, through which they have been delivered from so many burdens and troubles, and they might feel a little shame because, like pigs and dogs, they remember no more of the Gospel than this rotten,

---

[1] In the German edition of the Book of Concord, 1580, this Longer Preface (which dates from 1530) appeared after the Shorter Preface in accordance with the order observed in the fourth German volume of the Jena edition of Luther's Works (1556).

[2] Preachers (*Prediger*) were limited to preaching; pastors (*Pfarrherren*) exercised the full ministerial office.

[3] Titles of medieval sermon books.

[4] The seven canonical hours, daily prayers prescribed by the medieval Breviary.

[5] Luther published the "Little Prayer Book" (*Betbüchlein*) in 1522 to replace Roman Catholic devotional books.

pernicious, shameful, carnal liberty. As it is, the common people   4
take the Gospel altogether too lightly, and even our utmost exertions
accomplish but little. What, then, can we expect if we are sluggish
and lazy, as we used to be under the papacy?

Besides, a shameful and insidious plague of security and bore-   5
dom has overtaken us. Many regard the Catechism as a simple, silly
teaching which they can absorb and master at one reading. After
reading it once they toss the book into a corner as if they are ashamed
to read it again. Indeed, even among the nobility there are some   6
louts and skinflints who declare that we can do without pastors and
preachers from now on because we have everything in books and can
learn it all by ourselves. So they blithely let parishes fall into decay,
and brazenly allow both pastors and preachers to suffer distress and
hunger. This is what one can expect of crazy Germans. We Germans
have such disgraceful people among us and must put up with them.

As for myself, let me say that I, too, am a doctor and a preacher   7
—yes, and as learned and experienced as any of those who act so
high and mighty. Yet I do as a child who is being taught the Catechism. Every morning, and whenever else I have time, I read and
recite word for word the Lord's Prayer, the Ten Commandments, the
Creed, the Psalms, etc. I must still read and study the Catechism   8
daily, yet I cannot master it as I wish, but must remain a child and
pupil of the Catechism, and I do it gladly. These dainty, fastidious
fellows would like quickly, with one reading, to become doctors above
all doctors, to know all there is to be known. Well, this, too, is a
sure sign that they despise both their office and the people's souls, yes,
even God and his Word. They need not fear a fall, for they have
already fallen all too horribly. What they need is to become children
and begin learning their ABC's, which they think they have outgrown
long ago.

Therefore, I beg these lazy-bellies and presumptuous saints,   9
for God's sake, to get it into their heads that they are not really and
truly such learned and great doctors as they think. I implore them
not to imagine that they have learned these parts of the Catechism
perfectly, or at least sufficiently, even though they think they know
them ever so well. Even if their knowledge of the Catechism were
perfect (though that is impossible in this life), yet it is highly profitable
and fruitful daily to read it and make it the subject of meditation and
conversation. In such reading, conversation, and meditation the Holy
Spirit is present and bestows ever new and greater light and fervor, so
that day by day we relish and appreciate the Catechism more greatly.
This is according to Christ's promise in Matt. 18:20, "Where two or
three are gathered in my name, there am I in the midst of them."

Nothing is so effectual against the devil, the world, the flesh,   10
and all evil thoughts as to occupy oneself with the Word of God, talk

about it, and meditate on it. Psalm 1 calls those blessed who "meditate on God's law day and night." [6] You will never offer up any incense or other savor more potent against the devil than to occupy yourself with God's commandments and words and to speak, sing, and meditate on them. This, indeed, is the true holy water, the sign which routs the devil and puts him to flight. [7]

For this reason alone you should eagerly read, recite, ponder, | | and practice the Catechism, even if the only blessing and benefit you obtain from it is to rout the devil and evil thoughts. For he cannot bear to hear God's Word. God's Word is not like some empty tale, such as the one about Dietrich of Bern, [8] but as St. Paul says in Rom. 1:16, it is "the power of God," indeed, the power of God which burns the devil and gives us immeasurable strength, comfort, and help.

Why should I waste words? Time and paper would fail me if I | 2 were to recount all the blessings that flow from God's Word. The devil is called the master of a thousand arts. What, then, shall we call God's Word, which routs and destroys this master of a thousand arts with all his wiles and might? It must, indeed, be master of more than a hundred thousand arts. Shall we frivolously despise this | 3 might, blessing, power, and fruit—especially we who would be pastors and preachers? If so, we deserve not only to be refused food but also to be chased out by dogs and pelted with dung. Not only do we need God's Word daily as we need our daily bread; we also must use it daily against the daily, incessant attacks and ambushes of the devil with his thousand arts.

If this were not enough to admonish us to read the Catechism | 4 daily, there is God's command. That alone should be incentive enough. Deut. 6:7, 8 solemnly enjoins that we should always meditate upon his precepts whether sitting, walking, standing, lying down, or rising, and keep them before our eyes and in our hands as a constant token and sign. Certainly God did not require and command this so solemnly without good reason. He knows our danger and need. He knows the constant and furious attacks and assaults of the devil. So he wishes to warn, equip, and protect us against them with good "armor" against their "flaming darts," [9] and with a good antidote against their evil infection and poison. O what mad, senseless | 5 fools we are! We must ever live and dwell in the midst of such mighty enemies as the devils, and yet we despise our weapons and armor, too lazy to give them a thought!

[6] Ps. 1:2.
[7] I.e., the Word of God really does what holy water was formerly believed to accomplish.
[8] Luther frequently cited the legend of Dietrich of Bern as an example of lies and fables.
[9] Eph. 6:11, 16.

Look at these bored, presumptuous saints who will not or can- 16
not read and study the Catechism daily. They evidently consider
themselves much wiser than God himself, and wiser than all his holy
angels, prophets, apostles, and all Christians! God himself is not
ashamed to teach it daily, for he knows of nothing better to teach,
and he always keeps on teaching this one thing without varying it
with anything new or different. All the saints know of nothing better
or different to learn, though they cannot learn it to perfection. Are we
not most marvelous fellows, therefore, if we imagine, after reading
or hearing it once, that we know it all and need not read or study it
any more? Most marvelous fellows, to think we can finish learning
in one hour what God himself cannot finish teaching! Actually, he is
busy teaching it from the beginning of the world to the end, and all
prophets and saints have been busy learning it and have always remained pupils, and must continue to do so.

This much is certain: anyone who knows the Ten Command- 17
ments perfectly knows the entire Scriptures. In all affairs and circumstances he can counsel, help, comfort, judge, and make decisions in
both spiritual and temporal matters. He is qualified to sit in judgment
upon all doctrines, estates, persons, laws, and everything else in the
world.

What is the whole Psalter but meditations and exercises based 18
on the First Commandment? Now, I know beyond a doubt that such
lazy-bellies and presumptuous fellows do not understand a single
Psalm, much less the entire Scriptures, yet they pretend to know and
despise the Catechism, which is a brief compend and summary of all
the Holy Scriptures.

Therefore, I once again implore all Christians, especially pastors 19
and preachers, not to try to be doctors prematurely and to imagine
that they know everything. Vain imaginations, like new cloth, suffer
shrinkage! Let all Christians exercise themselves in the Catechism
daily, and constantly put it into practice, guarding themselves with the
greatest care and diligence against the poisonous infection of such
security or vanity. Let them continue to read and teach, to learn and
meditate and ponder. Let them never stop until they have proved by
experience that they have taught the devil to death and have become
wiser than God himself and all his saints.

If they show such diligence, then I promise them—and their 20
experience will bear me out—that they will gain much fruit and God
will make excellent men of them. Then in due time they themselves
will make the noble confession that the longer they work with the
Catechism, the less they know of it and the more they have to learn.
Only then, hungry and thirsty, will they truly relish what now they
cannot bear to smell because they are so bloated and surfeited. To
this end may God grant his grace! Amen.

PREFACE[1]

This sermon has been undertaken for the instruction of children 1 and uneducated people. Hence from ancient times it has been called, in Greek, a "catechism"—that is, instruction for children. Its 2 contents represent the minimum of knowledge required of a Christian. Whoever does not possess it should not be reckoned among Christians nor admitted to a sacrament,[2] just as a craftsman who does not know the rules and practices of his craft is rejected and considered incompetent. For this reason young people should be thoroughly in- 3 structed in the various parts of the Catechism or children's sermons and diligently drilled in their practice.

Therefore, it is the duty of every head of a household to examine 4 his children and servants at least once a week and ascertain what they have learned of it, and if they do not know it, to keep them faithfully at it. I well remember the time when there were old people who 5 were so ignorant that they knew nothing of these things—indeed, even now we find them daily—yet they come to Baptism and the Sacrament of the Altar and exercise all the rights of Christians, although those who come to the sacrament ought to know more and have a fuller understanding of all Christian doctrine than children and beginners at school. As for the common people, however, we 6 should be satisfied if they learned the three parts[3] which have been the heritage of Christendom from ancient times, though they were rarely taught and treated correctly, so that all who wish to be Christians in fact as well as in name, both young and old, may be well-trained in them and familiar with them.

I. THE TEN COMMANDMENTS OF GOD

1. You shall have no other gods before me.   1
2. You shall not take the name of God in vain.   2
3. You shall keep the Sabbath day holy.   3
4. You shall honor father and mother.   4
5. You shall not kill.   5
6. You shall not commit adultery.   6
7. You shall not steal.   7
8. You shall not bear false witness against your neighbor.   8

[1] The Shorter Preface is based on a sermon of May 18, 1528 (*WA*, 30I:2).

[2] This was not only a proposal of Luther, but also a medieval prescription; cf. John Surgant, *Manuale Curatorum* (1502), etc.

[3] Ten Commandments, Creed, Lord's Prayer. From 1525 on catechetical instruction in Wittenberg was expanded to include material on Baptism and the Lord's Supper.

9. You shall not covet your neighbor's house.   9
10. You shall not covet his wife, man-servant, maid-servant, cattle,
   or anything that is his.[4]   10

II. THE CHIEF ARTICLES OF OUR FAITH

I believe in God, the Father almighty, maker of heaven and   11
earth:

And in Jesus Christ, his only Son, our Lord: who was conceived   12
by the Holy Spirit, born of the virgin Mary, suffered under Pontius
Pilate, was crucified, dead, and buried: he descended into hell, the
third day he rose from the dead, he ascended into heaven, and sits on
the right hand of God, the Father almighty, whence he shall come
to judge the living and the dead.

I believe in the Holy Spirit, the holy Christian church,[5] the   13
communion of saints, the forgiveness of sins, the resurrection of the
body, and the life everlasting. Amen.

III. THE PRAYER, OR OUR FATHER, WHICH CHRIST TAUGHT

Our Father who art in heaven, hallowed be thy name. Thy   14
kingdom come, thy will be done, on earth as it is in heaven. Give us
this day our daily bread; and forgive us our debts, as we also have
forgiven our debtors; and lead us not into temptation, but deliver us
from evil. For thine is the kingdom and the power and the glory,
forever. Amen.[6]

These are the most necessary parts of Christian instruction.   15
We should learn to repeat them word for word. Our children   16
should be taught the habit of reciting them daily when they rise in
the morning, when they go to their meals, and when they go to bed
at night; until they repeat them they should not be given anything
to eat or drink. Every father has the same duty to his household;   17
he should dismiss man-servants and maid-servants if they do not know
these things and are unwilling to learn them. Under no circum-   18
stances should a person be tolerated if he is so rude and unruly that
he refuses to learn these three parts in which everything contained in
Scripture is comprehended in short, plain, and simple terms, for   19
the dear fathers or apostles, whoever they were,[7] have thus summed
up the doctrine, life, wisdom, and learning which constitute the Christian's conversation, conduct, and concern.

[4] Ex. 20:2-17; cf. Deut. 5:6-21.

[5] The translation of *ecclesiam catholicam* by *eine christliche Kirche* was
common in fifteenth century Germany.

[6] Matt. 6:9-13; cf. Luke 11:2-4.

[7] Luther was not interested in defending the apostolic authorship of the
Creed.

When these three parts are understood, we ought also to know   20
what to say about the sacraments which Christ himself instituted,
Baptism and the holy Body and Blood of Christ, according to the
texts of Matthew and Mark at the end of their Gospels where they
describe how Christ said farewell to his disciples and sent them forth.

BAPTISM   21

"Go and teach all nations, and baptize them in the name of the
Father and of the Son and of the Holy Spirit" (Matt. 28:19). "He
who believes and is baptized will be saved; but he who does not believe
will be condemned" (Mark 16:16).

It is enough for an ordinary person to know this much about   22
Baptism from the Scriptures. The other sacrament may be dealt with
similarly, in short, simple words according to the text of St. Paul.

THE SACRAMENT [OF THE ALTAR]   23

"Our Lord Jesus Christ on the night when he was betrayed took
bread, gave thanks, and broke it and gave it to his disciples, saying,
'Take and eat, this is my body, which is given for you. Do this in
remembrance of me.'

"In the same way also the cup, after supper, saying, 'This cup is
the new testament in my blood, which is shed for you for the forgiveness of sins. Do this, as often as you drink it, in remembrance of me' "
(I Cor. 11:23-25).

Thus we have, in all, five parts covering the whole of Christian   24
doctrine, which we should constantly teach and require young people
to recite word for word. Do not assume that they will learn and retain
this teaching from sermons alone. When these parts have been   25
well learned, you may assign them also some Psalms or some hymns,[8]
based on these subjects, to supplement and confirm their knowledge.
Thus our youth will be led into the Scriptures so that they make
progress daily.

However, it is not enough for them simply to learn and repeat   26
these parts verbatim. The young people should also attend preaching,
especially at the time designated for the Catechism,[9] so that they may
hear it explained and may learn the meaning of every part. Then they
will also be able to repeat what they have heard and give a good,
correct answer when they are questioned, and thus the preaching will
not be without benefit and fruit. The reason we take such care to   27
preach on the Catechism frequently is to impress it upon our youth,
not in a lofty and learned manner but briefly and very simply, so that
it may penetrate deeply into their minds and remain fixed in their
memories.

[8] Luther himself wrote six hymns based on the parts of the Catechism.
[9] Preaching and instruction on the Catechism especially during Lent.

Now we shall take up the above-mentioned parts one by one   28
and in the plainest possible manner say about them as much as is
necessary.

[FIRST PART: THE TEN COMMANDMENTS]

I am the Lord your God.

THE FIRST COMMANDMENT

You shall have no other gods.

What does this mean for us?

We are to fear, love, and trust God
above anything else.

THE FIRST COMMANDMENT

"You shall have no other gods."

That is, you shall regard me alone as your God. What does this   1
mean, and how is it to be understood? What is it to have a god? What
is God?

Answer: A god is that to which we look for all good and in   2
which we find refuge in every time of need. To have a god is nothing
else than to trust and believe him with our whole heart. As I have
often said, the trust and faith of the heart alone make both God and
an idol. If your faith and trust are right, then your God is the   3
true God. On the other hand, if your trust is false and wrong, then
you have not the true God. For these two belong together, faith and
God. That to which your heart clings and entrusts itself is, I say,
really your God.

The purpose of this commandment, therefore, is to require true   4
faith and confidence of the heart, and these fly straight to the one
true God and cling to him alone. The meaning is: "See to it that
you let me alone be your God, and never seek another." In other
words: "Whatever good thing you lack, look to me for it and seek it
from me, and whenever you suffer misfortune and distress, come and
cling to me. I am the one who will satisfy you and help you out of
every need. Only let your heart cling to no one else."

This I must explain a little more plainly, so that it may be   5
understood and remembered, by citing some common examples of

failure to observe this commandment. Many a person thinks he has God and everything he needs when he has money and property; in them he trusts and of them he boasts so stubbornly and securely that he cares for no one. Surely such a man also has a god—mammon[1] by   6 name, that is, money and possessions—on which he fixes his whole heart. It is the most common idol on earth. He who has money and   7 property feels secure, happy, fearless, as if he were sitting in the midst of paradise. On the other hand, he who has nothing doubts and   8 despairs as if he never heard of God. Very few there are who are   9 cheerful, who do not fret and complain, if they do not have mammon. This desire for wealth clings and cleaves to our nature all the way to the grave.

So, too, if anyone boasts of great learning, wisdom, power,   10 prestige, family, and honor, and trusts in them, he also has a god, but not the one, true God. Notice, again, how presumptuous, secure, and proud people become because of such possessions, and how despondent when they lack them or are deprived of them. Therefore, I repeat, to have a God properly means to have something in which the heart trusts completely.

Again, consider what we used to do in our blindness under the   11 papacy. If anyone had a toothache, he fasted to the honor of St. Apollonia; if he feared fire, he sought St. Lawrence as his patron; if he feared the plague, he made a vow to St. Sebastian or Roch.[2] There were countless other such abominations, and every person selected his own saint and worshiped and invoked him in time of need. In this   12 class belong those who go so far as to make a pact with the devil in order that he may give them plenty of money, help them in love affairs, protect their cattle, recover lost possessions, etc., as magicians and sorcerers do. All these fix their heart and trust elsewhere than in the true God. They neither expect nor seek anything from him.

Thus you can easily understand the nature and scope of this   13 commandment. It requires that man's whole heart and confidence be placed in God alone, and in no one else. To have God, you see, does not mean to lay hands upon him, or put him into a purse, or shut him up in a chest. We lay hold of him when our heart embraces him   14 and clings to him. To cling to him with all our heart is nothing   15 else than to entrust ourselves to him completely. He wishes to turn us

---

[1] Cf. Matt. 6:24.

[2] On Feb. 9, 248 or 249, Apollonia was martyred, her teeth being knocked out; the medieval church therefore considered her a help against toothache. Lawrence was martyred by burning on Aug. 10, 258. Sebastian was put to death by arrows on Jan. 20, early in the fourth century (?). Roch, who died in 1327, gave himself to care for plague victims. Cf. Luther's first extended exposition of the Ten Commandments (1518) for references to these and other saints, and to magicians and sorcerers. Contemporaries of Luther such as Erasmus also ridiculed this cult of saints.

away from everything else, and to draw us to himself, because he is the one, eternal good. It is as if he said: "What you formerly sought from the saints, or what you hoped to receive from mammon or anything else, turn to me for all this; look upon me as the one who wishes to help you and to lavish all good upon you richly."

Behold, here you have the true honor and the true worship which 16 please God and which he commands under penalty of eternal wrath, namely, that the heart should know no other consolation or confidence than that in him, nor let itself be torn from him, but for him should risk and disregard everything else on earth. On the other hand, 17 you can easily judge how the world practices nothing but false worship and idolatry. There has never been a people so wicked that it did not establish and maintain some sort of worship. Everyone has set up a god of his own, to which he looked for blessings, help, and comfort.

For example, the heathen who put their trust in power and 18 dominion exalted Jupiter as their supreme god. Others who strove for riches, happiness, pleasure, and a life of ease venerated Hercules, Mercury, Venus, or others, while pregnant women worshiped Diana or Lucina,[3] and so forth. Everyone made into a god that to which his heart was inclined. Even in the mind of all the heathen, therefore, to have a god means to trust and believe. The trouble is that their 19 trust is false and wrong, for it is not founded upon the one God, apart from whom there is truly no god in heaven or on earth. Accordingly the heathen actually fashion their fancies and dreams 20 about God into an idol and entrust themselves to an empty nothing. So it is with all idolatry. Idolatry does not consist merely of 21 erecting an image and praying to it. It is primarily in the heart, which pursues other things and seeks help and consolation from creatures, saints, or devils. It neither cares for God nor expects good things from him sufficiently to trust that he wants to help, nor does it believe that whatever good it receives comes from God.

There is, moreover, another false worship. This is the greatest 22 idolatry that has been practiced up to now, and it is still prevalent in the world. Upon it all the religious orders are founded. It concerns only that conscience which seeks help, comfort, and salvation in its own works and presumes to wrest heaven from God. It keeps account how often it has made endowments, fasted, celebrated Mass, etc. On such things it relies and of them it boasts, unwilling to receive anything as a gift from God, but desiring by itself to earn or merit everything by works of supererogation, just as if God were in our service or debt and we were his liege lords. What is this but making God into an 23 idol—indeed, an "apple-god"[4]—and setting up ourselves as God? This

[3] Lucina was the Roman goddess of birth, often identified with Juno.
[4] "Apfelgott" is possibly a corruption of "Aftergott," sham god. Luther speaks of "Apfelkönige oder gemalete Herrn" (WA, 31I:234), the latter

reasoning, however, is a little too subtle to be understood by young pupils.

This much, however, should be said to ordinary people so that   24
they may mark well and remember the meaning of this commandment: We are to trust in God alone and turn to him, expecting from him only good things; for it is he who gives us body, life, food, drink, nourishment, health, protection, peace, and all temporal and eternal blessings. It is he who protects us from evil, he who saves and delivers us when any evil befalls. It is God alone, I have often enough repeated, from whom we receive all that is good and by whom we are delivered from all evil. This, I think, is why we Germans   25
from ancient times have called God by a name more elegant and worthy than any found in other languages, a name derived from the word "good" [5] because he is an eternal fountain which overflows with sheer goodness and pours forth all that is good in name and in fact.

Although much that is good comes to us from men, we receive   26
it all from God through his command and ordinance. Our parents and all authorities—in short, all people placed in the position of neighbors—have received the command to do us all kinds of good. So we receive our blessings not from them, but from God through them. Creatures are only the hands, channels, and means through which God bestows all blessings. For example, he gives to the mother breasts and milk for her infant, and he gives grain and all kinds of fruits from the earth for man's nourishment—things which no creature could produce by himself. No one, therefore, should presume to   27
take or give anything except as God has commanded it. We must acknowledge everything as God's gifts and thank him for them, as this commandment requires. Therefore, this way of receiving good through God's creatures is not to be disdained, nor are we arrogantly to seek other ways and means than God has commanded, for that would be not receiving our blessings from God but seeking them from ourselves.

Let everyone, then, take care to magnify and exalt this   28
commandment above all things and not make light of it. Search and examine your own heart thoroughly and you will find whether or not it clings to God alone. Do you have the kind of heart that expects from him nothing but good, especially in distress and want, and renounces and forsakes all that is not God? Then you have the one true God. On the contrary, does your heart cling to something else, from which it hopes to receive more good and help than from God, and does it flee not to him but from him when things go wrong? Then you have an idol, another god.

expression, literally "painted lords," being a term of derision somewhat like "plaster saint." Sebastian Franck uses the term *"Apfelkaiser."* The *"Apfelbischof"* was a Shrove Tuesday character in parts of Germany.

   [5] Luther asserted this derivation more than once. But the two words, both in old German and in Gothic, are not etymologically connected.

Consequently, in order to show that God will not have this 29
commandment taken lightly but will strictly watch over it, he has
attached to it, first, a terrible threat and, then, a beautiful, comforting
promise. These should be thoroughly stressed and impressed upon
young people so that they may take them to heart and remember them.

[EXPLANATION OF THE APPENDIX TO THE FIRST COMMANDMENT][6]

"For I am the Lord your God, mighty and jealous, visiting the 30
iniquity of the fathers upon the children to the third and fourth
generation of those who hate me, and showing mercy to many
thousands of those who love me and keep my commandments." [7]

Although these words apply to all the commandments (as we 31
shall hear later),[8] yet they are attached precisely to this one which
stands at the head of the list because it is of the utmost importance
for a man to have the right head. For where the head is right, the
whole life must be right, and vice versa. Learn from these words, 32
then, how angry God is with those who rely on anything but himself,
and again, how kind and gracious he is to those who trust and believe
him alone with their whole heart. His wrath does not abate until the
fourth generation. On the other hand, his kindness and goodness 33
extend to many thousands, lest men live in security and commit themselves to luck, like brutes who think that it makes no great difference
how they live. He is a God who takes vengeance upon men who 34
turn away from him, and his anger continues to the fourth generation,
until they are utterly exterminated. Therefore he wills to be feared
and not to be despised.

This he has witnessed in all the records of history, as Scripture 35
amply shows and as daily experience can still teach us. From the
beginning he has completely rooted out all idolatry, and on that
account he has destroyed both heathen and Jews; just so in our day
he overthrows all false worship so that all who persist in it must
ultimately perish. Even now there are proud, powerful, and rich 36
pot-bellies who, not caring whether God frowns or smiles, boast
defiantly of their mammon and believe that they can withstand his
wrath. But they will not succeed. Before they know it they will be
wrecked, along with all they have trusted in, just as all others have
perished who thought themselves to be so high and mighty.

Just because such blockheads imagine, when God refrains from 37
disturbing their security, that he is unconcerned or uninterested in

---

[6] This subtitle is found only in the Latin version.
[7] This text is virtually the same as in Luther's Bible translation at Exod.
20:5. An entirely different German rendering appears in the conclusion of
his exposition of the Ten Commandments, below, 320.
[8] See below, Ten Commandments, 321, 326.

such matters, he must strike and punish them so severely that he will not forget his anger down to their children's children. He intends that everyone shall be impressed and see that this is no laughing matter with him. These are also the people he means when he says, 38 "who hate me," that is, those who persist in their stubbornness and pride. They refuse to hear what is preached or spoken to them. When they are rebuked, to bring them to their senses and cause them to mend their ways before punishment descends, they become so mad and foolish that they justly merit the wrath they receive. We observe this every day in the case of bishops and princes.

Terrible as these threats are, much mightier is the comfort in 39 the promise that assures mercy to those who cling to God alone—sheer goodness and blessing, not only for themselves but also for their children to a thousand and even many thousands of generations. Certainly, if we desire all good things in time and eternity, this 40 ought to move and impel us to fix our hearts upon God with perfect confidence since the divine Majesty comes to us with so gracious an offer, so cordial an invitation, and so rich a promise.

Therefore let everyone be careful not to regard this as if it 41 were spoken by man. For it brings you either eternal blessing, happiness, and salvation, or eternal wrath, misery, and woe. What more could you ask or desire than God's gracious promise that he will be yours with every blessing and will protect and help you in every need? The trouble is that the world does not believe this at all, 42 and does not recognize it as God's Word. For the world sees that those who trust God and not mammon suffer grief and want and are opposed and attacked by the devil. They have neither money, prestige, nor honor, and can scarcely even keep alive; meanwhile, those who serve mammon have power, prestige, honor, wealth, and every comfort in the eyes of the world. Accordingly, we must grasp these words, even in the face of this apparent contradiction, and learn that they neither lie nor deceive but will yet prove to be true.

Reflect on the past, search it out, and tell me, When men have 43 devoted all their care and diligence to scraping together great wealth and money, what have they gained in the end? You will find that they have wasted their effort and toil or, if they have amassed great treasures, that these have turned to dust and vanished. They themselves have never found happiness in their wealth, nor has it ever lasted to the third generation.[9] Examples of this you will find 44 aplenty in all histories and in the recollections of elderly and experienced people. Just ponder and heed them. Saul was a great king, 45

---

[9] A late Latin proverb, often quoted by Luther, declares: "Ill-gotten gains will not last to the third generation."

chosen by God, and an upright man; but once he was secure on his throne and he let his heart depart from God, placing his confidence in his crown and power, he inevitably perished with all that he had; not one of his children remained.[1] David, on the other hand, was   46 a poor, despised man, hunted down and persecuted, his life nowhere secure, yet inevitably he remained safe from Saul and became king.[2] These words must stand and prove to be true since God cannot lie or deceive; just leave it to the devil and the world to deceive you with their appearance, which indeed endures for a time but in the end is nothing! [3]

Let us therefore learn the first commandment well and realize   47 that God will tolerate no presumption and no trust in any other object; he makes no greater demand of us than a hearty trust in him for all blessings. Then we shall be on the right path and walk straight ahead, using all of God's gifts exactly as a cobbler uses his needle, awl, and thread (for work, eventually to lay them aside) or as a traveler avails himself of an inn, food, and bed (only for his temporal need). Let each person be in his station in life according to God's order, allowing none of these good things to be his lord or idol.

Let this suffice for the First Commandment. We had to explain   48 it at length since it is the most important. For, as I said before,[4] where the heart is right with God and this commandment is kept, fulfillment of all the others will follow of its own accord.

[1] Cf. I Sam. 10, 15, 16, 31; II Sam. 4.

[2] Cf. I Sam. 18 to II Sam. 2.

[3] The first Latin translator, Obsopoeus, and the German (1580) and Latin (1584) editions of the Book of Concord added a negative, thereby turning Luther's quip into a sober admonition.

[4] See above, Ten Commandments, 31.

THE SECOND COMMANDMENT

You shall not take the name of the Lord your God in vain.

What does this mean for us?

We are to fear and love God
so that we do not use his name
    superstitiously, or use it
to curse, swear, lie, or deceive,
but call on him in prayer, praise, and
    thanksgiving.

THE SECOND COMMANDMENT

"You shall not take the name of God in vain."   49

As the First Commandment has inwardly instructed the heart   50
and taught faith, so this commandment leads us outward and directs
the lips and the tongue into the right relation to God. The first things
that issue and emerge from the heart are words. As I have taught
above how to answer the question, What it is to have a God, so you
must learn to grasp simply the meaning of this and all the other
commandments and apply them to yourself.

If you are asked, "How do you understand the Second Com-   51
mandment? What does it mean to misuse or take the name of God in
vain?" you should answer briefly: "It is a misuse of God's name if we
call upon the Lord God in any way whatsoever to support falsehood or
wrong of any kind." Therefore what this commandment forbids is
appealing to God's name falsely or taking his name upon our lips
when our heart knows or should know that the facts are otherwise—
for example, where men take oaths in court and one side lies against
the other. God's name cannot be more grievously abused than for   52
purposes of falsehood and deceit. Let this stand as the plain and simple
meaning of this commandment.

From this everyone can readily infer when and in how many   53
ways God's name is abused, though it is impossible to enumerate all
its misuses. To discuss it briefly, misuse of the divine name occurs
most obviously in worldly business and in matters involving money,

property, and honor, whether publicly in court or in the market or elsewhere, when a person perjures himself, swearing by God's name or by his own soul. This is especially common in marriage matters when two persons secretly betroth themselves to each other and afterward deny it under oath.

The greatest abuse, however, occurs in spiritual matters, which   54 pertain to the conscience, when false preachers arise and peddle their lying nonsense as the Word of God.

See, all this is an attempt to embellish yourself with God's name   55 or to put up a good front and justify yourself, whether in ordinary worldly affairs or in sublime and difficult matters of faith and doctrine. Also to be counted among liars are blasphemers, not only the very crass ones who are well known to everyone and who disgrace God's name unabashedly (these belong in the hangman's school, not ours), but also those who publicly slander the truth and God's Word and consign it to the devil. Of this there is no need to speak further.

Let us take to heart how important this commandment is and   56 diligently shun and avoid every misuse of the holy name as the greatest sin that can be committed outwardly. For to lie and deceive is in itself a gross sin, but it is greatly aggravated when we attempt to justify and confirm it by invoking God's name and using it as a cloak to cover our shame. So from a single lie a double one results— indeed, manifold lies.

Therefore God has attached to this commandment a solemn   57 threat: "for the Lord will not hold him guiltless who takes his name in vain." This means that in no one shall a violation be condoned or left unpunished. As little as God will permit the heart that turns away from him to go unpunished, so little will he permit his name to be used to gloss over a lie. Unfortunately it is now a common   58 calamity all over the world that there are few who do not use the name of God for lies and all kinds of wickedness, just as there are few who trust in God with their whole heart.

By nature we all have this beautiful virtue that whenever we   59 commit a wrong we like to cover and gloss over our disgrace so that no one may see it or know it. No man is so arrogant as to boast before the whole world of the wickedness he has committed. We prefer to act in secret without anyone's being aware of it. Then if anyone is denounced, God and his name have to be dragged in to turn the villainy into righteousness and the disgrace into honor. This is the   60 common course of the world. Like a great deluge, it has flooded all lands. Hence we get what we deserve: plague, war, famine, fire, flood, wayward wives and children and servants, and troubles of every kind. Where else could so much misery come from? It is a great mercy that the earth still bears and sustains us.

Above all things, therefore, our young people should be strictly   61 required and trained to hold this as well as the other commandments in high regard. Whenever they transgress, we must be after them at once with the rod, confront them with the commandment, and continually impress it upon them, so that they may be brought up not merely with punishment but in the reverence and fear of God.

Now you understand what it means to take God's name in vain. 62 To repeat very briefly, it is either simply to lie and assert under his name something that is not so, or to curse, swear, conjure, and, in short, to practice wickedness of any sort.

In addition, you must also know how to use the name of God 63 aright. With the words, "You shall not take the name of God in vain," God at the same time gives us to understand that we are to use his name properly, for it has been revealed and given to us precisely for our use and benefit. Since we are forbidden here to use the 64 holy name in support of falsehood or wickedness, it follows, conversely, that we are commanded to use it in the service of truth and all that is good—for example, when we swear properly where it is necessary and required. So, also, when we teach properly; again, when we call on his name in time of need, or praise and thank him in time of prosperity, etc. All this is summarized in the command in Ps. 50:15, "Call upon me in the day of trouble: I will deliver you and you shall glorify me." All this is what we mean by calling upon his name in service of truth and using it devoutly. Thus his name is hallowed, as we pray in the Lord's Prayer.

Here you have the substance of the entire commandment 65 explained. If it is so understood, you have easily solved the question that has tormented so many teachers:[5] why swearing is forbidden in the Gospel,[6] and yet Christ, St. Paul,[7] and other saints took oaths. The explanation is briefly this: We are not to swear in support of 66 evil (that is, to a falsehood) or unnecessarily; but in support of the good and for the advantage of our neighbor we are to swear. This is a truly good work by which God is praised, truth and justice are established, falsehood is refuted, people are reconciled, obedience is rendered, and quarrels are settled. For here God himself intervenes and separates right from wrong, good from evil. If one party in 67 a dispute swears falsely, he will not escape punishment. Though it may take a long time, nothing he does will in the end succeed; everything he may gain by the false oath will slip through his fingers and will never be enjoyed. This I have seen in the case of many who broke their 68

---

[5] E.g., Augustine and Jerome. The issue had taken on new urgency with the rise of the Anabaptists.

[6] Matt. 5:33-37.

[7] Matt. 26:63f.; Gal. 1:20; II Cor. 1:23.

promise of marriage; they never enjoyed a happy hour or a healthful day thereafter, and thus they miserably perished, body, soul, and possessions.

Therefore I advise and urge, as I have before, that by means   69
of warning and threat, restraint and punishment, children be trained in due time to shun falsehood and especially to avoid calling upon God's name in its support. Where they are allowed to do as they please, no good will come of it. It is evident that the world today is more wicked than it has ever been. There is no government, no obedience, no fidelity, no faith—only perverse, unbridled men whom no teaching or punishment can help. All this is God's wrath and punishment upon such willful contempt of this commandment.

On the other hand, children should be constantly urged and   70
encouraged to honor God's name and keep it constantly upon their lips in all circumstances and experiences, for true honor to God's name consists of looking to it for all consolation and therefore calling upon it. Thus, as we have heard above, the heart by faith first gives God the honor due him and then the lips do so by confession.

This is a blessed and useful habit, and very effective against the   71
devil, who is ever around us, lying in wait to lure us into sin and shame, calamity and trouble. He hates to hear God's name and cannot long remain when it is uttered and invoked from the heart. Many a   72
terrible and shocking calamity would befall us if God did not preserve us through our calling upon his name. I have tried it myself and learned by experience that often sudden, great calamity was averted and vanished in the very moment I called upon God. To defy the devil, I say, we should always keep the holy name on our lips so that he may not be able to injure us as he is eager to do.

For this purpose it also helps to form the habit of commending   73
ourselves each day to God—our soul and body, wife, children, servants, and all that we have—for his protection against every conceivable need. Thus has originated and continued among us the custom of saying grace and returning thanks at meals and saying other prayers for both morning and evening.[8] From the same source came the   74
custom of children who cross themselves when they see or hear anything monstrous or fearful and exclaim, "Lord God, save us!" "Help, dear Lord Christ!" etc. Thus, too, if anyone meets with unexpected good fortune, however trivial, he may say, "God be praised and thanked!" "This God has bestowed upon me!" etc. Children used to be trained to fast and pray to St. Nicholas and other

---

[8] See the blessing before meals, the thanksgiving after meals, and the morning and evening blessings appended at the end of the Small Catechism, above.

saints, but the other practices would be more pleasing and acceptable to God than any monastic life and Carthusian holiness.[9]

With childish and playful methods like these we may bring up   75 our youth in the fear and honor of God so that the First and Second Commandments may become familiar and be constantly practiced. Then some good may take root, spring up, and bear fruit, and men may grow up of whom an entire land may be proud. This would be   76 the right way to bring up children, so long as they can be trained with kind and pleasant methods, for those who have to be forced by means of rods and blows will come to no good end; at best they will remain good only as long as the rod is on their backs.

This kind of training takes such root in their hearts that they   77 fear God more than they do rods and clubs. This I say plainly for the sake of the young, so that it may sink into their minds, for when we preach to children, we must also speak their language. Thus we have averted the misuse of the divine name and taught that its right use consists not only of words but also of practice and life. We want them to know that God is well pleased with the right use of his name and will as richly reward it, even as he will terribly punish its misuse.

[9] Luther often cited the Carthusian Order (founded 1084) as an example of particularly strict asceticism and self-devised holiness.

THE THIRD COMMANDMENT

Remember the Sabbath day, to
keep it holy.

What does this mean for us?

We are to fear and love God
so that we do not neglect his Word
    and the preaching of it,
but regard it as holy
and gladly hear and learn it.

THE THIRD COMMANDMENT

"You shall sanctify the holy day."   78

Our word "holy day" or "holiday" is so called from the Hebrew   79
word "Sabbath," which properly means to rest, that is, to cease from
labor; hence our common expression for "stopping work" literally
means "observing a holy day or holiday." [1] In the Old Testament   80
God set apart the seventh day and appointed it for rest, and he
commanded it to be kept holy above all other days.[2] As far as outward
observance is concerned, the commandment was given to the Jews
alone. They were to abstain from hard work and to rest, so that both
man and beast might be refreshed and not be exhausted by constant
labor. In time, however, the Jews interpreted this commandment   81
too narrowly and grossly misused it. They slandered Christ and would
not permit him to do what they themselves were in the habit of doing
on that day, as we read in the Gospel[3]—as if the commandment

---

[1] The ambiguity in the German word *Feiertag,* to which Luther refers, is
discernible in the connection between the English words "holy day" and
"holiday." *Feiren (feiern)* means to celebrate a festival, or simply to take
time off from work. *Feierabend machen* or *heiligen Abend geben,* common
expressions for "taking (or granting) time off," literally mean observing (or
granting) a holy day, originally the eve of a festival.

[2] Gen. 2:3.

[3] Matt. 12:1ff.; Mark 2:23ff.; Luke 6:1ff, 13:10ff., 14:1ff.; John 5:9ff.,
7:22f., 9:14ff.

could be fulfilled by refraining from manual labor of any kind. This was not its intention, but, as we shall hear, it meant that we should sanctify the holy day or day of rest.

Therefore, according to its literal, outward sense, this com-   82
mandment does not concern us Christians. It is an entirely external matter, like the other ordinances of the Old Testament connected with particular customs, persons, times, and places,[4] from all of which we are now set free through Christ.[5]

To offer ordinary people a Christian interpretation of what   83
God requires in this commandment, we point out that we keep holy days not for the sake of intelligent and well informed Christians, for these have no need of them. We keep them, first, for the sake of bodily need. Nature teaches and demands that the common people—man-servants and maid-servants who have attended to their work and trades the whole week long—should retire for a day to rest and be refreshed. Secondly and most especially, we keep holy days so   84
that people may have time and opportunity, which otherwise would not be available, to participate in public worship, that is, that they may assemble to hear and discuss God's Word and then praise God with song and prayer.

This, I say, is not restricted to a particular time, as it was among   85
the Jews, when it had to be precisely this or that day, for in itself no one day is better than another. Actually, there should be worship daily; however, since this is more than the common people can do, at least one day in the week must be set apart for it. Since from ancient times Sunday has been appointed for this purpose, we should not change it. In this way a common order will prevail and no one will create disorder by unnecessary innovation.

This, then, is the plain meaning of this commandment: Since   86
we observe holidays anyhow, we should devote their observance to learning God's Word. The special office of this day, therefore, should be the ministry of the Word for the sake of the young and the poor common people. However, the observance of rest should not be so narrow as to forbid incidental and unavoidable work.

Accordingly, when you are asked what "You shall sanctify the   87
holy day" means, answer: "It means to keep it holy." What is meant by "keeping it holy"? Nothing else than to devote it to holy words, holy works, holy life. In itself the day needs no sanctification, for it

---

[4] In his treatise "Against the Heavenly Prophets" (1525) Luther argued that whatever in the Mosaic Law exceeds the natural law is strictly binding on the Jews alone. The Mosaic Law is "the Jews' 'Saxon Code.'" France does not observe the Saxon Code, except in so far as it agrees with its own laws on the common ground of the natural law. Man's need for a day of rest is a testimony of nature. Just so, Christ placed the Sabbath law under man, Matt. 12, Mark 3 (*WA*, 18:81, 82).

[5] Cf. Col. 2:16f.

was created holy. But God wants it to be holy to you. So it becomes holy or unholy on your account, according as you spend the day in doing holy or unholy things.

How does this sanctifying take place? Not when we sit behind 88 the stove and refrain from external work, or deck ourselves with garlands and dress up in our best clothes, but, as has been said, when we occupy ourselves with God's Word and exercise ourselves in it.

Indeed, we Christians should make every day a holy day and 89 give ourselves only to holy activities—that is, occupy ourselves daily with God's Word and carry it in our hearts and on our lips. However, as we have said, since all people do not have this much time and leisure, we must set apart several hours a week for the young, and at least a day for the whole community, when we can concentrate upon such matters and deal especially with the Ten Commandments, the Creed, and the Lord's Prayer. Thus we may regulate our whole life and being according to God's Word. Wherever this practice is in 90 force, a holy day is truly kept. Where it is not, it cannot be called a Christian holy day. Non-Christians can spend a day in rest and idleness, too, and so can the whole swarm of clerics in our day who stand daily in the churches, singing and ringing bells, without sanctifying the holy day because they neither preach nor practice God's Word but teach and live contrary to it.

The Word of God is the true holy thing[6] above all holy things. 91 Indeed, it is the only one we Christians acknowledge and have. Though we had the bones of all the saints or all the holy and consecrated vestments gathered together in one heap, they could not help us in the slightest degree, for they are all dead things that can sanctify no one. But God's Word is the treasure that sanctifies all things. By it all the saints themselves have been sanctified. At whatever time God's 92 Word is taught, preached, heard, read, or pondered, there the person, the day, and the work are sanctified by it, not on account of the external work but on account of the Word which makes us all saints. Accordingly, I constantly repeat that all our life and work must be guided by God's Word if they are to be God-pleasing or holy. Where that happens the commandment is in force and is fulfilled.

Conversely, any conduct or work done apart from God's Word 93 is unholy in the sight of God, no matter how splendid and brilliant it may appear, or even if it be altogether covered with holy relics, as are the so-called spiritual estates[7] who do not know God's Word but seek holiness in their own works.

---

[6] *Heiligtum* is the word for "relic." To understand Luther's meaning, read something like this: We used to be taught to revere relics and other "holy things." But the Word of God is the true holy thing, etc.

[7] Cf. the title of Luther's treatise, "Against the Falsely So-called Spiritual Estate of the Pope and the Bishops" (1522).

Note, then, that the power and force of this commandment   94
consist not of the resting but of the sanctifying, so that this day
should have its own particular holy work. Other trades and occupations
are not properly called holy work unless the doer himself is first holy.
But here a work must be performed by which the doer himself is made
holy; this, as we have heard, takes place only through God's Word.
Places, times, persons, and the entire outward order of worship are
therefore instituted and appointed in order that God's Word may
exert its power publicly.

Since so much depends on God's Word that no holy day is   95
sanctified without it, we must realize that God insists upon a strict
observance of this commandment and will punish all who despise his
Word and refuse to hear and learn it, especially at the times appointed.

Therefore this commandment is violated not only by those who   96
grossly misuse and desecrate the holy day, like those who in their
greed or frivolity neglect to hear God's Word or lie around in taverns
dead drunk like swine, but also by that multitude of others who listen
to God's Word as they would to any other entertainment, who only
from force of habit go to hear preaching and depart again with as little
knowledge of the Word at the end of the year as at the beginning.
It used to be thought that Sunday had been properly hallowed if   97
one heard a Mass or the reading of the Gospel; no one asked about
God's Word, and no one taught it either. Now that we have God's
Word, we still fail to remove the abuse of the holy day, for we permit
ourselves to be preached to and admonished but we listen without
serious concern.

Remember, then, that you must be concerned not only about   98
hearing the Word but also about learning and retaining it. Do not
regard it as an optional or unimportant matter. It is the commandment
of God, and he will require of you an accounting of how you have
heard and learned and honored his Word.

In the same way those conceited fellows should be chastised   99
who, after hearing a sermon or two, become sick and tired of it and
feel that they know it all and need no more instruction. This is
precisely the sin that used to be classed among the mortal sins and was
called *acidia*[8]—that is, indolence or satiety—a malignant, pernicious
plague with which the devil bewitches and befuddles the hearts of many
so that he may take us by surprise and stealthily take the Word of God
away from us.

Let me tell you this. Even though you know the Word perfectly   100
and have already mastered everything, still you are daily under the
dominion of the devil, who neither day nor night relaxes his effort to
steal upon you unawares and to kindle in your heart unbelief and

---

[8] The term *acedia* (or *acidia*) comes from Aristotle's Ethics, Book IV.

wicked thoughts against all these commandments. Therefore you must continually keep God's Word in your heart, on your lips, and in your ears. For where the heart stands idle and the Word is not heard, the devil breaks in and does his damage before we realize it. On the |101| other hand, when we seriously ponder the Word, hear it, and put it to use, such is its power that it never departs without fruit. It always awakens new understanding, new pleasure, and a new spirit of devotion, and it constantly cleanses the heart and its meditations. For these words are not idle or dead, but effective and living. Even if no |102| other interest or need drove us to the Word, yet everyone should be spurred on by the realization that in this way the devil is cast out and put to flight, this commandment is fulfilled, and God is more pleased than by any work of hypocrisy, however brilliant.

THE FOURTH COMMANDMENT

Honor your father and your mother.

What does this mean for us?

We are to fear and love God
so that we do not despise or anger our
    parents and others in authority,
but respect, obey, love, and serve them.

THE FOURTH COMMANDMENT

Thus far we have learned the first three commandments, which   103
are directed toward God. First, we should trust, fear, and love him
with our whole heart all the days of our lives. Secondly, we should not
misuse his holy name in support of lies or any evil purpose whatsoever,
but use it for the praise of God and the benefit and salvation of our
neighbor and ourselves. Thirdly, on holy days or days of rest we
should diligently devote ourselves to God's Word so that all our
conduct and life may be regulated by it. Now follow the other seven,
which relate to our neighbor. Among these the first and greatest is:

"You shall honor your father and mother."   104

To fatherhood and motherhood God has given the special   105
distinction, above all estates that are beneath it, that he commands us
not simply to love our parents but also to honor them. With respect
to brothers, sisters, and neighbors in general he commands nothing
higher than that we love them. Thus he distinguishes father and
mother above all other persons on earth, and places them next to
himself. For it is a much greater thing to honor than to love.   106
Honor includes not only love but also deference, humility, and
modesty, directed (so to speak) toward a majesty hidden within them.
It requires us not only to address them affectionately and   107
reverently, but above all to show by our actions, both of heart and of
body, that we respect them very highly and that next to God we give
them the very highest place. For anyone whom we are whole-heartedly
to honor, we must truly regard as high and great.

Young people must therefore be taught to revere their parents   108
as God's representatives, and to remember that, however lowly, poor,
feeble, and eccentric they may be, they are their own father and
mother, given them by God. They are not to be deprived of their
honor because of their ways or their failings. Therefore, we are not
to think of their persons, whatever they are, but of the will of God,

who has created and ordained them to be our parents. In other respects, indeed, we are all equal in the sight of God, but among ourselves there must be this sort of inequality and proper distinctions. God therefore commands you to be careful to obey me as your father and to acknowledge my authority.

First, then, learn what this commandment requires concerning 109 honor to parents. You are to esteem and prize them as the most precious treasure on earth. In your words you are to behave 110 respectfully toward them, and not address them discourteously, critically, and censoriously, but submit to them and hold your tongue, even if they go too far. You are also to honor them by your 111 actions (that is, with your body and possessions), serving them, helping them, and caring for them when they are old, sick, feeble, or poor; all this you should do not only cheerfully, but with humility and reverence, as in God's sight. He who has the right attitude toward his parents will not allow them to suffer want or hunger, but will place them above himself and at his side and will share with them all he has to the best of his ability.

In the second place, notice what a great, good, and holy work 112 is here assigned to children. Alas, it is utterly despised and brushed aside, and no one recognizes it as God's command or as a holy, divine word and precept. For if we had regarded it as such, it would have been apparent to all that they who lived according to these words must also be holy men. Then there would have been no need to institute monasticism or "spiritual estates." Every child would have remained faithful to this commandment and would have been able to set his conscience right toward God, saying: "If I am to do good and holy works, I know of none better than to show all honor and obedience to my parents, since God himself has commanded it. What God commands must be much nobler than anything we 113 ourselves may devise. And because there is no greater or better teacher to be found than God, there can also be no better teaching than his. Now, he amply teaches what we should do if we wish to perform truly good works, and by commanding them he shows that he is well pleased with them. So, if this is God's command, and it embodies his highest wisdom, then I shall never improve upon it."

In this way, you see, we should have had godly children, 114 properly taught, and reared in true blessedness; they would have remained at home in obedience and service to their parents, and we should have had an object lesson in goodness and happiness. However, men did not feel obliged to set forth God's commandment in its full glory. They were able to ignore it and skip lightly over it, and so children could not lay it to heart; they simply gaped in astonishment at all the arrangements we have devised without ever asking God's approval.

For the love of God, therefore, let us at last teach our young   115
people to banish all other things from sight and give first place to this
commandment. If they wish to serve God with truly good works, they
must do what is pleasing to their fathers and mothers, or to those
who have parental authority over them. Every child who knows and
does this has, in the first place, the great comfort of being able
joyfully to boast in the face of all who are occupied with works of
their own choice: "See, this work is well pleasing to my God in
heaven; this I know for certain." Let them all come forward   116
and boast of their many great, laborious, and difficult works; we shall
see whether they can produce a single work that is greater and nobler
than obedience to father and mother, which God has appointed and
commanded next to obedience to his own majesty. If God's Word
and will are placed first and observed, nothing ought to be considered
more important than the will and word of our parents, provided that
these, too, are subordinated to obedience toward God and are not set
into opposition to the preceding commandments.

You should rejoice heartily and thank God that he has chosen   117
and fitted you to perform a task so precious and pleasing to him.
Even though it seems very trivial and contemptible, make sure that you
regard it as great and precious, not on account of your worthiness but
because it has its place within that jewel and holy treasure, the Word
and commandment of God. O how great a price all the   118
Carthusian monks and nuns[9] would pay if in the exercise of their
religion they could bring before God a single work done in accordance
with his commandment and could say with a joyful heart in his
presence, "Now I know that this work is well pleasing to Thee!"
What will become of these poor wretched people when, standing before
God and the whole world, they shall blush with shame before a little
child that has lived according to this commandment and confess that
with the merits of their whole lives they are not worthy to offer him
a cup of water? It serves them right for their devilish perversity   119
in trampling God's commandment under foot that they must torture
themselves in vain with their self-devised works[1] and meanwhile have
only scorn and trouble for their reward.

Should not the heart leap and melt with joy when it can go to   120
work and do what is commanded, saying, "Lo, this is better than the
holiness of all the Carthusians, even though they kill themselves with
fasting and pray on their knees without ceasing"? Hence you have a
sure text and a divine testimony that God has commanded this;

---

[9] Here and elsewhere the translator of the Latin version, Obsopoeus,
altered "Carthusians" into "Carmelites," a hermit order founded *ca.* 1180
on Mt. Carmel in Palestine, later transformed into a mendicant order.

[1] Self-appointed works in contrast to God's commands—for example, the
injunction to strict silence, avoidance of meat, extreme vigils, etc.

concerning the other things he has commanded not a word. This is the plight and the miserable blindness of the world that no one believes this; so thoroughly has the devil bewitched us with the false holiness and glamor of our own works.

Therefore, I repeat, I should be very glad if we were to open 121 our eyes and ears and take this to heart so that we may not again be led astray from the pure Word of God to the lying vanities of the devil. Then all would be well; parents would have more happiness, love, kindness, and harmony in their houses, and children would win their parents' hearts completely. On the other hand, when they 122 are obstinate and never do their duty until a rod is laid on their backs, they anger both God and their parents. Thus they deprive themselves of this treasure and joy of conscience and lay up for themselves nothing but misfortune. That is the way things go in the world 123 now, as everyone complains. Both young and old are altogether wayward and unruly; they have no sense of modesty or honor; they do nothing until they are driven with blows; and they defame and depreciate one another behind their backs in any way they can. God therefore punishes them so that they sink into all kinds of trouble and misery. Neither can parents, as a rule, do very much; one 124 fool trains another, and as they have lived, so live their children after them.

This, I say, should be the first and strongest reason impelling 125 us to keep this commandment. If we had no father and mother, we should wish, on account of the commandments, that God would set up a block or a stone which we might call father and mother. How much more, when he has given us living parents, should we be happy to show them honor and obedience. For we know that it is highly pleasing to the divine Majesty and all the angels, that it vexes all devils, and, besides, that it is the greatest work that we can do, next to the sublime worship of God described in the previous commandments. Even 126 almsgiving and all other works for our neighbor are not equal to this. For God has exalted this estate of parents above all others; indeed, he has appointed it to be his representative on earth. This will and pleasure of God ought to provide us sufficient reason and incentive to do cheerfully and gladly whatever we can.

Besides this, it is our duty before the world to show gratitude 127 for the kindness and for all the good things we have received from our parents. But here again the devil rules in the world; children 128 forget their parents, as we all forget God, and no one takes thought how God feeds, guards, and protects us and how many blessings of body and soul he bestows upon us. Especially when an evil hour comes do we rage and grumble impatiently and forget all the blessings **we have received throughout our life. Just so we act toward our** parents, and there is no child that recognizes and considers this, unless he is led to it by the Holy Spirit.

The perversity of the world God knows very well. By means of 129 commandments, therefore, he reminds and impels everyone to consider what his parents have done for him. Then everybody recognizes that he has received his body and life from them and that he has been nourished and nurtured by them when otherwise he would have perished a hundred times in his own filth. The wise men of old 130 were right when they said, "God, parents, and teachers can never be sufficiently thanked and repaid." [2] He who views the matter in this light will, without compulsion, give all honor to his parents and esteem them as those through whom God has given him all blessings.

Over and above all this, another strong incentive for us to 131 keep this commandment is that God has attached to it a lovely promise, "That you may have long life in the land where you dwell." Here you see how important God considers this commandment. 132 He declares that it is not only an object of pleasure and delight to himself, but also an instrument intended for our greatest welfare, to lead us to a quiet, pleasant, and blessed life. St. Paul also highly 133 exalts and praises this commandment, saying in Eph. 6:2, 3, "This is the first commandment with a promise: that it may be well with you and that you may live long on the earth." Although the other commandments also have a promise implied, yet in none is it so plainly and explicitly stated.

This, then, is the fruit and the reward, that whoever keeps 134 this commandment will enjoy good days, happiness, and prosperity. On the other hand, the penalty for him who disobeys it is that he will perish sooner and never be happy in life. For, in the Scriptures, to have long life means not merely to grow old but to have everything that pertains to long life—health, wife and child, livelihood, peace, good government, etc., without which this life can neither be heartily enjoyed nor long endure. If you are unwilling to obey father and 135 mother or to submit to them, then obey the hangman; and if you will not obey him, then obey the grim reaper,[3] Death! This, in short, 136 is the way God will have it: render him obedience and love and service, and he will reward you abundantly with every blessing; on the other hand, if you provoke him to anger, he will send upon you both death and the hangman.

[2] Cf. *WA,* 30^{II}:579: "A diligent, upright schoolteacher or master, or anyone who faithfully trains and teaches boys, can never be sufficiently repaid, as the pagan Aristotle says."

[3] Luther often used the word *Streckebein,* primarily a Low German expression for death. A parallel word is *Streckefuss.* A seventeenth century explanation is that in mortal illness the legs give out before the head, i.e., the dying man is stretched out on his bed. Obsopoeus translated the word with *carnifex,* executioner.

Why do we have so many criminals who must daily be hanged, |37 beheaded, or broken on the wheel if not because of disobedience? They will not allow themselves to be brought up in kindness; consequently, by the punishment of God they bring upon themselves the misfortune and grief that we behold, for it seldom happens that such wicked people die a natural and timely death.

The godly and the obedient, however, are blessed. They live long in peace and quietness. They see their children's children, as we said above, "to the third and fourth generation." Again, as we know |38 from experience, where there are fine old families who prosper and have many children, it is certainly because some of them were brought up well and revered their parents. On the other hand, it is written of the wicked in Ps. 109:13, "May his posterity be cut off: and may their name be cut off in one generation." Learn well, then, how |39 important God considers obedience, since he so highly exalts it, so greatly delights in it, so richly rewards it, and besides is so strict about punishing those who transgress it.

All this I say that it may be thoroughly impressed upon the |40 young people, for no one will believe how necessary is this commandment, which in the past was neither heeded nor taught under the papacy. These are plain and simple words, and everyone thinks he already knows them well. So he passes over them lightly, fastens his attention on other things, and fails to perceive and believe how angry he makes God when he neglects this commandment, and how precious and acceptable a work he does when he observes it.

In connection with this commandment there is more to be said |41 about the various kinds of obedience due to our superiors, persons whose duty it is to command and to govern. Out of the authority of parents all other authority is derived and developed. Where a father is unable by himself to bring up his child, he calls upon a schoolmaster to teach him; if he is too weak, he enlists the help of his friends and neighbors; if he passes away, he confers and delegates his authority and responsibility to others appointed for the purpose. Likewise he must have domestics (man-servants and |42 maid-servants) under him to manage the household. Thus all who are called masters stand in the place of parents and derive from them their power and authority to govern. In the Scriptures they are all called fathers because in their responsibility they act in the capacity of fathers and ought to have fatherly hearts toward their people. So from ancient times the Romans and other peoples called the masters and mistresses of the household *patres et matres familias* (that is, house-fathers and house-mothers). Again, their princes and overlords were called *patres patriae*[4] (that is, fathers of the country) to the

---

[4] Cicero received this title after exposing the conspiracy of Catiline. In later times it became a part of the Roman emperor's official title.

great shame of us would-be Christians who do not speak of our rulers in the same way, or at least do not treat and honor them as such.

What a child owes to father and mother, the entire household 143 owes them likewise. Therefore man-servants and maid-servants should take care not only to obey their masters and mistresses, but also to honor them as their own parents and do everything that they know is expected of them, not from compulsion and reluctantly but gladly and cheerfully; and they should do it for the reason just mentioned, that it is God's commandment and is more pleasing to him than all other works. They ought even to be willing to pay for the privilege of 144 service and be glad to acquire masters and mistresses in order to have such joyful consciences and know how to do truly golden works. These works in the past have been neglected and despised; instead, everybody ran in the devil's name into monasteries, on pilgrimages, and after indulgences, to their own hurt and with a bad conscience.

If this truth could be impressed upon the poor people, a 145 servant girl would dance for joy and praise and thank God; and with her careful work, for which she receives sustenance and wages, she would gain a treasure such as all who pass for the greatest saints do not have. Is it not a wonderful thing to be able to boast to yourself, "If I do my daily housework faithfully, that is better than the holiness and austere life of all the monks"? You have the promise, 146 moreover, that you will prosper and fare well in everything. How can you lead a more blessed or holy life, as far as your works are concerned? In the sight of God it is really faith that makes a 147 person holy; faith alone serves him, while our works serve the people. Here you have everything that is good—shelter and protection 148 in the Lord and, what is more, a joyful conscience and a gracious God who will reward you a hundredfold. You are a true nobleman if you are upright and obedient. If you are not, you will have nothing but the wrath and displeasure of God; there will be no peace in your heart, and eventually you will have all kinds of trouble and misfortune.

Whoever will not be moved by this, and who will not be 149 inclined to godliness, we deliver to the hangman and the grim reaper. Therefore, let everyone who can take advice remember that God is not to be taken lightly. God speaks to you and demands obedience. If you obey him you are his dear child; if you despise this command-ment, then take shame, misery, and grief for your reward.

The same may be said of obedience to the civil government, 150 which, as we have said, is to be classed with the estate of fatherhood, the most comprehensive of all relations. In this case a man is father not of a single family, but of as many people as he has inhabitants, citizens, or subjects. Through civil rulers, as through our own parents, God gives us food, house and home, protection and security. Therefore, since they bear this name and title with all honor as their chief glory, it is our duty to honor and magnify them as the most precious treasure and jewel on earth.

He who is obedient, willing, ready to serve, and cheerfully |51 gives honor where it is due, knows that he pleases God and receives joy and happiness for his reward. On the other hand, if he will not do so in love, but despises or rebelliously resists authority, let him know that he shall have no favor or blessing from God. Where he counts on gaining a gulden[5] by his unfaithfulness, he will lose ten elsewhere. Or he will fall victim to the hangman, or perish through war, pestilence, or famine, or his children will turn out badly; servants, neighbors, or strangers and tyrants will inflict injury, injustice, and violence upon him. What we seek and deserve, then, is paid back to us in retaliation.

If we ever let ourselves be persuaded that works of obedience |52 are so pleasing to God and have so rich a reward, we shall be simply overwhelmed with our blessings and we shall have all that our hearts desire. But God's Word and commandment are despised, as if they came from some loutish peddler. Let us see, though, whether you are the man to defy him. How difficult do you think it will be for him to pay you back? You will live much better with God's favor, |53 peace, and blessing than you will with disfavor and misfortune. Why, do you think, is the world now so full of unfaithfulness, |54 shame, misery, and murder? It is because everyone wishes to be his own master, be free from all authority, care nothing for anyone, and do whatever he pleases. So God punishes one knave by means of another. When you defraud or despise your master, another person comes along and treats you likewise. Indeed, in your own household you must suffer ten times as much wrong from your own wife, children, or servants.

Of course, we keenly feel our misfortune, and we grumble and |55 complain of unfaithfulness, violence, and injustice; but we are unwilling to see that we ourselves are knaves who have roundly deserved punishment and that we are not one bit improved by it. We spurn favor and happiness; therefore, it is only fair that we have nothing but unhappiness without mercy. Somewhere on earth there must |56 still be some godly people, or else God would not grant us so many blessings! If it depended on our merits, we would not have a penny[6] in the house or a straw in the field. All this I have been obliged |57 to set forth with such a profusion of words in the hope that someone may take it to heart, so that we may be delivered from the blindness and misery in which we are so deeply sunk and may rightly understand

---

[5] The gulden was originally a large gold coin, later also silver, the equivalent of a florin.

[6] In popular expressions the heller, or penny, represented extreme insignificance in contrast with the groschen and other coins.

the Word and will of God and sincerely accept it. From God's Word we could learn how to obtain an abundance of joy, happiness, and salvation, both here and in eternity.

Thus we have three kinds of fathers presented in this com- |58 mandment: fathers by blood, fathers of a household, and fathers of the nation. Besides these, there are also spiritual fathers—not like those in the papacy who applied this title to themselves but performed no fatherly office. For the name spiritual father belongs only to those who govern and guide us by the Word of God. St. Paul boasts |59 that he is a father in I Cor. 4:15, where he says, "I became your father in Christ Jesus through the Gospel." Since such persons are |60 fathers, they are entitled to honor, even above all others. But they very seldom receive it, for the world's way of honoring them is to harry them out of the country and grudge them as much as a piece of bread. In short, as St. Paul says, they must be "the refuse of the world, and every man's offscouring." [7]

Yet there is need to impress upon the common people that |6| they who would bear the name of Christians owe it to God to show "double honor" [8] to those who watch over their souls and to treat them well and make provision for them. God will adequately recompense those who do so and will not let them suffer want. But here everybody resists and rebels; all are afraid that their |62 bellies will suffer, and therefore they cannot now support one good preacher although in the past they filled ten fat paunches. For |63 this we deserve to have God deprive us of his Word and his blessings and once again allow preachers of lies[9] to arise and lead us to the devil—and wring sweat and blood out of us besides.

Those who keep their eyes on God's will and commandment, |64 however, have the promise that they will be richly rewarded for all they contribute to their temporal and spiritual fathers, and for the honor they render them. Not only shall they have bread, clothing, and money for a year or two, but long life, sustenance, and peace, and afterwards abundance and blessedness forever. Do your duty, |65 then, and leave it to God how he will support you and provide for all your wants. Since he has promised it, and has never yet lied, he will not lie to you either.

This ought to encourage us and make our hearts so melt for |66 joy and love toward those to whom we owe honor that we lift our hands in joyful thanks to God for giving us such promises. We ought to be willing to run to the ends of the world to obtain them. For the

[7] I Cor. 4:13.
[8] I Tim. 5:17.
[9] "Preachers of lies" (cf. Mic. 2:11) was a favorite epithet in the sixteenth century.

combined efforts of the whole world cannot add an hour to our life
or raise from the earth a single grain of wheat for us. But God can
and will give you everything abundantly, according to your heart's
desire. He who despises and disdains this is not worthy to hear a word
from God.

More than enough has now been said to those to whom this
commandment applies.

In addition, it would be well to preach to parents on the nature 167
of their office, how they should treat those committed to their
authority. Although the duty of superiors is not explicitly stated in
the Ten Commandments, it is frequently dealt with in many other
passages of Scripture, and God intends it to be included in this
commandment in which he speaks of father and mother. God 168
does not want to have knaves or tyrants in this office and responsibility;
nor does he assign them this honor (that is, power and authority to
govern) merely to receive homage. Parents should consider that they
owe obedience to God, and that, above all, they should earnestly and
faithfully discharge the duties of their office, not only to provide for
the material support of their children, servants, subjects, etc., but
especially to bring them up to the praise and honor of God.
Therefore do not imagine that the parental office is a matter of 169
your pleasure and whim. It is a strict commandment and injunction
of God, who holds you accountable for it.

The trouble is that no one perceives or heeds this. Everybody 170
acts as if God gave us children for our pleasure and amusement, gave
us servants merely to put them to work like cows or asses, and gave us
subjects to treat them as we please, as if it were no concern of ours
what they learn or how they live. No one is willing to see that 171
this is the command of the divine Majesty, who will solemnly call us to
account and punish us for its neglect, nor is it recognized how very
necessary it is to devote serious attention to the young. If we 172
want qualified and capable men for both civil and spiritual leadership,
we must spare no effort, time, and expense in teaching and educating
our children to serve God and mankind. We must not think only of
amassing money and property for them. God can provide for 173
them and make them rich without our help, as indeed he does daily.
But he has given and entrusted children to us with the command that
we train and govern them according to his will; otherwise God would
have no need of father and mother. Therefore let everybody 174
know that it is his chief duty, on pain of losing divine grace, to bring
up his children in the fear and knowledge of God, and if they are
gifted to give them opportunity to learn and study so that they may
be of service wherever they are needed.

If this were done, God would richly bless us and give us grace 175
so that men might be trained who would be a benefit to the nation

and the people. We would also have soundly instructed citizens,
virtuous and home-loving wives who would faithfully bring up their
children and servants to be godly. Think what deadly harm you |76
do when you are negligent in this respect and fail to bring up your
children to usefulness and piety. You bring upon yourself sin and
wrath, thus earning hell by the way you have reared your own
children, no matter how devout and holy you may be in other respects.
Because this commandment is disregarded, God terribly punishes |77
the world; hence there is no longer any civil order, peace, or respect
for authority. We all complain about this state of things, but we do
not see that it is our own fault. Because of the way we train them,
we have unruly and disobedient subjects.

This is enough to serve as a warning; a more extensive |78
explanation will have to await another occasion.[1]

[1] Soon after this Luther wrote his "Sermon on Keeping Children in School"
(1530).

THE FIFTH COMMANDMENT

You shall not kill.

What does this mean for us?

We are to fear and love God
so that we do not hurt our neighbor in
   any way,
but help him in all his physical needs.

THE FIFTH COMMANDMENT

"You shall not kill."   179

We have now dealt with both the spiritual and the civil govern-   180
ment, that is, divine and paternal authority and obedience. In this
commandment we leave our own house and go out among our neighbors to learn how we should conduct ourselves individually toward our
fellow men. Therefore neither God nor the government is included in
this commandment, yet their right to take human life is not abrogated.
God has delegated his authority of punishing evil-doers to civil   181
magistrates in place of parents; in early times, as we read in Moses,[2]
parents had to bring their own children to judgment and sentence them
to death. Therefore what is forbidden here applies to private individuals,
not to governments.

This commandment is simple enough. We hear it explained   182
every year in the Gospel, Matthew 5,[3] where Christ himself explains
and summarizes it: We must not kill, either by hand, heart, or word,
by signs or gestures, or by aiding and abetting. It forbids anger
except, as we have said, to persons who occupy the place of God,
that is, parents and rulers. Anger, reproof, and punishment are the
prerogatives of God and his representatives, and they are to be
exercised upon those who transgress this and the other commandments.

The occasion and need for this commandment is that, as God   183
well knows, the world is evil and this life is full of misery. He has
therefore placed this and the other commandments as a boundary
between good and evil. There are many offenses against this command-

[2] Deut. 21:18-20.

[3] Matt. 5:20-26 is the Gospel for the sixth Sunday after Trinity. We have
16 sermons of Luther on this text.

ment, as there are against all the others. We must live among many
people who do us harm, and so we have reason to be at enmity with
them. For instance, a neighbor, envious that you have received |84
from God a better house and estate or greater wealth and good fortune
than he, gives vent to his irritation and envy by speaking ill of you.

Thus by the devil's prompting you acquire many enemies who
begrudge you even the least good, whether physical or spiritual.
When we see such people, our hearts in turn rage and we are ready
to shed blood and take revenge. Then follow cursing and blows, and
eventually calamity and murder. Here God, like a kind father, |85
steps in and intervenes to get the quarrel settled for the safety of all
concerned. Briefly, he wishes to have all people defended, delivered,
and protected from the wickedness and violence of others, and he has
set up this commandment as a wall, fortress, and refuge about our
neighbor so that no one may do him bodily harm or injury.

What this commandment teaches, then, is that no one should |86
harm another for any evil deed, no matter how much he deserves it.
Not only is murder forbidden, but also everything that may lead to
murder. Many persons, though they may not actually commit murder,
nevertheless call down curses and imprecations upon their enemy's
head, which, if they came true, would soon put an end to him.
This spirit or revenge clings to every one of us, and it is common |87
knowledge that no one willingly suffers injury from another. Therefore
God wishes to remove the root and source of this bitterness toward
our neighbor. He wants us to keep this commandment ever before our
eyes as a mirror in which to see ourselves, so that we may be attentive
to his will and with hearty confidence and prayer commit to him
whatever wrong we suffer. Then we shall be content to let our enemies
rave and rage and do their worst. Thus we may learn to calm our
anger and have a patient, gentle heart, especially toward those who
have given us occasion for anger, namely, our enemies.

Briefly, then, to impress it unmistakably upon the common |88
people, the import of the commandment against killing is this: In the
first place, we should not harm anyone. This means, first, by hand
or by deed; next, we should not use our tongue to advocate or advise
harming anyone; again, we should neither use nor sanction any means
or methods whereby anyone may be harmed; finally, our heart should
harbor no hostility or malice toward anyone in a spirit of anger and
hatred. Thus you should be blameless toward all people in body and
soul, especially toward him who wishes or does you evil. For to do
evil to somebody who desires and does you good is not human but
devilish.

In the second place, this commandment is violated not only |89
when a person actually does evil, but also when he fails to do good to
his neighbor, or, though he has the opportunity, fails to prevent, protect,

and save him from suffering bodily harm or injury. If you send   190
a person away naked when you could clothe him, you have let him
freeze to death. If you see anyone suffer hunger and do not feed him,
you have let him starve. Likewise, if you see anyone condemned[4] to
death or in similar peril and do not save him although you know ways
and means to do so, you have killed him. It will do you no good to
plead that you did not contribute to his death by word or deed, for
you have withheld your love from him and robbed him of the service
by which his life might have been saved.

Therefore God rightly calls all persons murderers who do not   191
offer counsel and aid to men in need and in peril of body and life. He
will pass a most terrible sentence upon them in the day of judgment,
as Christ himself declares. He will say: "I was hungry and thirsty
and you gave me no food or drink, I was a stranger, and you did not
welcome me, I was naked and you did not clothe me, I was sick and in
prison, and you did not visit me." [5] That is to say, "You would have
permitted me and my followers to die of hunger, thirst, and cold, to be
torn to pieces by wild beasts, to rot in prison or perish from want."

What else is this but to reproach such persons as murderers and   192
bloodhounds? For although you have not actually committed all these
crimes, as far as you were concerned you have nevertheless permitted
your neighbor to languish and perish in his misfortune.

It is just as if I saw someone wearily struggling in deep water, or
fallen into a fire, and could extend him my hand to pull him out and
save him, and yet I did not do it. How would I appear before all the
world in any other light than as a murderer and a scoundrel?

Therefore it is God's real intention that we should allow no   193
man to suffer harm, but show to everyone all kindness and love.
And this kindness is directed, as I said, especially toward our   194
enemies. To show kindness to our friends is but an ordinary heathen
virtue, as Christ says in Matthew 5:46, 47.

Here again we have God's Word by which he wants to   195
encourage and urge us to true, noble, exalted deeds, such as gentleness,
patience, and, in short, love and kindness toward our enemies. He
always wants to remind us to think back to the First Commandment,
that he is our God; that is, he wishes to help and protect us, so that he
may subdue our desire for revenge.

If this could be thoroughly impressed on people's minds, we   196
would have our hands full of good works to do. But this would   197
be no preaching for monks. It would too greatly undermine the
"spiritual estate" and infringe upon the holiness of the Carthusians. It
would be practically the same as forbidding their good works and

---

[4] Variant reading: innocently condemned.
[5] Matt. 25:42, 43.

emptying the monasteries. For in this teaching an ordinary Christian life would be considered just as acceptable, and even more so. Everybody would see how the monks mock and mislead the world with a false, hypocritical show of holiness, while they have thrown this and the other commandments to the winds, regarding them as unnecessary, as if they were not commandments but mere counsels.[6] Moreover, they have shamelessly boasted and bragged of their hypocritical calling and works as "the most perfect life," so that they might live a nice, soft life without the cross and suffering. This is why they fled to the monasteries, so that they might not have to suffer wrong from anyone or do anyone any good. Know, however, that it is the works |98 commanded by God's Word which are the true, holy, and divine works in which he rejoices with all the angels. In contrast to them all human holiness is only stench and filth, and it merits nothing but wrath and damnation.

[6] Luther here is making a sarcastic play on the Roman Catholic distinction between "commandments" and "(evangelical) counsels" according to which all men are unconditionally obligated to keep the "commandments," but a voluntary observance of the "counsels" brings special grace while their non-observance is no sin.

THE SIXTH COMMANDMENT

You shall not commit adultery.

What does this mean for us?

We are to fear and love God
so that in matters of sex our words and
    conduct are pure and honorable,
and husband and wife love and respect
    each other.

THE SIXTH COMMANDMENT

"You shall not commit adultery."   199

The following commandments are easily understood from the   200
preceding one. They all teach us to guard against harming our neighbor
in any way. They are admirably arranged. First they deal with our
neighbor's person. Then they proceed to the person nearest and
dearest to him, namely, his wife, who is one flesh and blood with him.[7]
In no possession of his can we inflict a greater injury upon him.
Therefore, it is explicitly forbidden here to dishonor his wife.
Adultery is particularly mentioned because among the Jewish   201
people marriage was obligatory. Youths were married at the earliest
age possible. The state of virginity was not commended, neither were
public prostitution and lewdness tolerated as they are now. Accordingly adultery was the most common form of unchastity among them.

Inasmuch as there is a shameful mess and cesspool of all   202
kinds of vice and lewdness among us, this commandment applies to
every form of unchastity, however it is called. Not only is the external
act forbidden, but also every kind of cause, motive, and means. Your
heart, your lips, and your whole body are to be chaste and to afford
no occasion, aid, or encouragement to unchastity. Moreover,   203
you are to defend, protect, and rescue your neighbor whenever he is in
danger or need, and on the contrary to aid and assist him so that he
may retain his honor. Whenever you fail to do this (though you   204
could prevent a wrong) or wink at it as if it were no concern of yours,

[7] Cf. Gen. 2:24.

you are just as guilty as the culprit himself. In short, everyone   205
is required both to live chastely himself and to help his neighbor do
the same. Thus God by his commandment wants every husband or
wife guarded and protected from any trespass.

Inasmuch as this commandment is concerned specifically with   206
the estate of marriage and gives occasion to speak of it, let us
carefully note, first, how highly God honors and glorifies the married
life, sanctioning and protecting it by his commandment. He sanctioned
it above in the fourth commandment, "You shall honor father and
mother"; but here, as I said, he has secured it and protected it.
Therefore he also wishes us to honor, maintain, and cherish it   207
as a divine and blessed estate. Significantly he established it as the
first of all institutions, and he created man and woman differently
(as is evident) not for lewdness but to be true to each other, be
fruitful, beget children, and support and bring them up to the glory
of God.

God has therefore most richly blessed this estate above all   208
others and, in addition, has supplied and endowed it with everything
in the world in order that this estate might be provided for richly and
adequately. Married life is no matter for jest or idle curiosity, but
it is a glorious institution and an object of God's serious concern.
For it is of the highest importance to him that persons be brought up
to serve the world, promote knowledge of God, godly living, and all
virtues, and fight against wickedness and the devil.

Therefore I have always taught that we should not despise or   209
disdain marriage, as the blind world and the false clergy do, but view
it in the light of God's Word, by which it is adorned and sanctified.
It is not an estate to be placed on a level with the others; it precedes
and surpasses them all, whether those of emperor, princes, bishops, or
anyone else. Important as the spiritual and civil estates are, these
must humble themselves and allow all people to enter the estate of
marriage, as we shall hear. It is not an exceptional estate, but   210
the most universal and the noblest, pervading all Christendom and
even extending throughout all the world.

In the second place, remember that it is not only an honorable   211
estate but also a necessary one, and it is solemnly commanded by God
that in general men and women in all conditions, who have been
created for it, shall be found in this estate. Yet there are some
(although few) exceptions whom God has especially exempted—some
who are unsuited for married life and others whom he has released by
a high supernatural gift so that they can maintain chastity outside of
marriage. Where nature has its way, as God implanted it, it is not   212
possible to remain chaste outside of marriage; for flesh and blood
remain flesh and blood, and the natural inclinations and stimulations
have their way without let or hindrance, as everyone's observation and

experience testify. Therefore, to make it easier for man to avoid unchastity in some measure, God has established marriage, so that everyone may have his allotted portion and be satisfied with it— although here, too, God's grace is still required to keep the heart pure.

From this you see how the papal rabble, priests, monks, and 2 I 3 nuns resist God's order and commandment when they despise and forbid marriage, and boast and vow that they will maintain perpetual chastity while they deceive the common people with lying words and wrong impressions. For no one has so little love and inclination 2 I 4 for chastity as those who under the guise of great sanctity avoid marriage and either indulge in open and shameless fornication or secretly do even worse—things too evil to mention, as unfortunately has been only too well proved. In short, even though they 2 I 5 abstain from the act, yet their hearts remain so full of unchaste thoughts and evil desires that they suffer incessant ragings of secret passion, which can be avoided in married life. Therefore all vows 2 I 6 of chastity apart from marriage are condemned and annulled by this commandment; indeed, all poor, captive consciences deceived by their monastic vows are even commanded to forsake their unchaste existence and enter the married life. Even granting that the monastic life is godly, yet it is not in their power to maintain chastity, and if they remain they will inevitably sin more and more against this commandment.

I say these things in order that our young people may be led 2 I 7 to acquire a love for married life and know that it is a blessed and God-pleasing estate. Thus it may in due time regain its proper honor, and there may be less of the filthy, dissolute, disorderly conduct which now is so rampant everywhere in public prostitution and other shameful vices resulting from contempt of married life. Therefore 2 I 8 parents and magistrates have the duty of so supervising youth that they will be brought up to decency and respect for authority and, when they are grown, will be married honorably in the fear of God. Then God will add his blessing and grace so that men may have joy and happiness in their married life.

Let it be said in conclusion that this commandment requires 2 I 9 everyone not only to live chastely in thought, word, and deed in his particular situation (that is, especially in the estate of marriage), but also to love and cherish the wife or husband whom God has given. For marital chastity it is above all things essential that husband and wife live together in love and harmony, cherishing each other whole-heartedly and with perfect fidelity. This is one of the chief ways to make chastity attractive and desirable. Under such conditions chastity always follows spontaneously without any command. This is why 220 St. Paul so urgently admonishes husbands and wives to love and honor

each other.[8] Here you have another precious good work—indeed,   22 |
many and great works—which you can joyfully set over against all
"spiritual estates" that are chosen without God's Word and
commandment.

[8] Cf. Eph. 5:22, 25; Col. 3:18f.

THE SEVENTH COMMANDMENT

You shall not steal.

What does this mean for us?

> We are to fear and love God
> so that we do not take our neighbor's
>   money or property,
> or get them in any dishonest way,
> but help him to improve and protect
> his property and means of making a
>   living.

THE SEVENTH COMMANDMENT

"You shall not steal."   222

Next to our own own person and our spouse, our temporal   223
property is dearest to us. This, too, God wants to have protected. He
has forbidden us to rob or pilfer the possessions of our neighbor.
For to steal is nothing else than to acquire another's property by   224
unjust means. In a few words, this includes taking advantage of our
neighbor in any sort of dealing that results in loss to him. Stealing is a
widespread, common vice, but people pay so little attention to it that
the matter is entirely out of hand. If all who are thieves, though they
are unwilling to admit it, were hanged on the gallows, the world would
soon be empty, and there would be a shortage of both hangmen and
gallows. As I have just said, a person steals not only when he robs a
man's strongbox or his pocket, but also when he takes advantage of
his neighbor at the market, in a grocery shop, butcher stall, wine- and
beer-cellar, work-shop, and, in short, wherever business is transacted
and money is exchanged for goods or labor.

Let us make it a little clearer for the common people so that   225
we may see how honest we are. Suppose, for example, that a man-
servant or maid-servant is unfaithful in his or her domestic duty and
does damage or permits damage to happen when it could have been
avoided. Or suppose that through laziness, carelessness, or malice a
servant wastes and neglects things to the vexation and annoyance of
his master or mistress. When this is done deliberately—for I am not
speaking of what happens inadvertently and unintentionally—a servant
can cheat his employer out of thirty or forty gulden or more a year.
If a thief had taken such sums he would be strangled with a noose,

but the servant may even become defiant and insolent and dare anyone to call him a thief!

The same must be said of artisans, workmen, and day-laborers 226 who act high-handedly and never know enough ways to overcharge people and yet are careless and unreliable in their work. All these are far worse than sneak-thieves, against whom we can guard with lock and bolt, or if we catch them we can deal with them so that they will not repeat the offense. But against the others no one can guard. No one even dares to give them a hard look or accuse them of theft. One would ten times rather lose the money from one's purse. For these are my neighbors, my good friends, my own servants, from whom I expect good; but they are the first to defraud me.

Furthermore, at the market and in everyday business the same 227 fraud prevails in full force. One person openly cheats another with defective merchandise, false measures, dishonest weights, and bad coins, and takes advantage of him by underhanded tricks and sharp practices and crafty dealing. Or again, one swindles another in a trade and deliberately fleeces, skins, and torments him. Who can even describe or imagine it all? In short, thievery is the most common 228 craft and the largest guild on earth. If we look at mankind in all its conditions, it is nothing but a vast, wide stable full of great thieves.

These men are called gentleman swindlers[9] or big operators. 229 Far from being picklocks and sneak-thieves who loot a cash box, they sit in office chairs and are called great lords and honorable, good citizens, and yet with a great show of legality they rob and steal.

Yes, we might well keep quiet here about various petty 230 thieves in order to launch an attack against the great, powerful arch-thieves who consort with lords and princes and daily plunder not only a city or two, but all Germany. Indeed, what would become of the head and chief protector of all thieves, the Holy See at Rome, and all its retinue, which has plundered and stolen the treasures of the whole world and holds them to this day?

This, in short, is the way of the world. Those who can steal 231 and rob openly are safe and free, unmolested by anyone, even claiming honor from men. Meanwhile the little sneak-thieves who have committed one offense must bear disgrace and punishment so as to make the others look respectable and honorable. But the latter should be told that in the eyes of God they are the greatest thieves, and that he will punish them as they deserve.

This commandment is very far-reaching, as we have shown. It 232

---

[9] Luther's word is *Stuhlräuber,* a contemporary expression for "usurers." He takes the term to refer to men whom we might call "swivel-chair operators." Luther's etymology, however, is wrong; *Stuhlräuber* is derived not from *Stuhl,* meaning chair, but from the Low German *Stôl,* meaning capital let out for interest or "rent."

is necessary, therefore, to emphasize and explain it to the common people in order that they may be restrained in their wantonness and that the wrath of God may be continually and urgently kept before their eyes. For we must preach this not to Christians but chiefly to knaves and scoundrels, though it might be more fitting if the judge, the jailer, or the hangman did the preaching. Let every one 233 know, then, that it is his duty, at the risk of God's displeasure, not to harm his neighbor, take advantage of him, or defraud him by any faithless or underhanded business transaction. More than that, he is under obligation faithfully to protect his neighbor's property and further his interests, especially when he takes remuneration for such services.

A person who willfully disregards this commandment may 234 indeed get by and escape the hangman, but he will not escape God's wrath and punishment. Though he pursues his defiant and arrogant course for a long time, still he will remain a tramp and a beggar and will suffer all kinds of troubles and misfortunes. Now, you 235 servants ought to take care of your master's or mistress's property, which enables you to stuff your craw and your belly. But you go your own way, take your wages like a thief, and even expect to be revered like noblemen. Many of you are even insolent toward masters and mistresses and unwilling to do them the favor and service of protecting them from loss. But see what you gain. When you come into 236 property yourself and have a house of your own—which God will let you acquire to your undoing—there will come a day of reckoning and retribution: for every penny you have taken and for every penny's damage you have done you will have to pay back thirty-fold.

So will it be with artisans and day-laborers, from whom we are 237 obliged to suffer such intolerable insolence. They act as if they were lords over others' possessions and entitled to whatever they demand. Just let them keep on boldly fleecing people as long as they can. 238 God will not forget his commandment. He will pay them what they deserve. He will hang them not on a green gallows but on a dry one.[1] They will neither prosper nor gain anything their whole life long. Of course, if our government were well regulated, such insolence 239 might soon be checked. The ancient Romans, for example, promptly took such offenders by the scruff of the neck so that others took warning.

The same fate will overtake those who turn the free public 240 market into a carrion-pit and a robbers' den. Daily the poor are defrauded. New burdens and high prices are imposed. Everyone misuses the market in his own willful, conceited, arrogant way, as if it

---

[1] Death on the gallows was considered a more ignominious punishment than death on a green tree ("green gallows").

were his right and privilege to sell his goods as dearly as he pleases
without a word of criticism. We shall stand by and let such   241
persons fleece, grab, and hoard. But we shall trust God, who   242
takes matters into his own hands. After they have scrimped and scraped
for a long time, he will pronounce this kind of blessing over them:
"Your grain will spoil in the garner and your beer in the cellar. Your
cattle will die in the stall. Yes, where you have cheated and defrauded
anyone out of a gulden, your entire hoard will be consumed by rust
so that you will never enjoy it."

Indeed, we have the evidence before our very eyes every day   243
that no stolen or ill-gotten possession thrives. How many people scrape
and scratch day and night and yet grow not a penny richer! Though
they gather a great hoard, they must suffer so many troubles and
misfortunes that they can never enjoy it or pass it on to their children.
But because we ignore this and act as if it were none of our   244
business, God must punish us and teach us morals in a different way.
He lays on us one affliction after another, or he quarters a troop of
soldiers upon us; in one hour they clean out our chests and purse down
to the last penny, and then by way of thanks they burn and ravage
house and home and outrage and kill wife and children.

In short, however much you steal, depend on it that just as   245
much will be stolen from you. Anyone who robs and takes things by
violence and dishonesty must put up with another who plays the same
game. For God is a master of this art; since everyone robs and steals
from the other, he punishes one thief by means of another. Otherwise,
where would we find enough gallows and ropes?

Whoever is willing to learn a lesson, let him know that this   246
is God's commandment and must not be treated as a joke. We shall
put up with those of you who despise, defraud, steal, and rob us. We
shall endure your arrogance and show forgiveness and mercy, as the
Lord's Prayer teaches. The upright, meanwhile, will not want, and you
will hurt yourself more than others. But beware how you deal with
the poor, of whom there are many now. If, when you meet a   247
poor man who must live from hand to mouth, you act as if everyone
must live by your favor, you skin and scrape him right down to the
bone, and you arrogantly turn him away whom you ought to give aid,
he will go away wretched and dejected, and because he can complain
to no one else, he will cry to heaven. Beware of this, I repeat, as
of the devil himself. Such a man's sighs and cries will be no joking
matter. They will have an effect too heavy for you and all the world
to bear, for they will reach God, who watches over poor, sorrowful
hearts, and he will not leave them unavenged. But if you despise and
defy this, see whom you have brought upon yourself. If you succeed
and prosper, before all the world you may call God and me liars.

We have now given sufficient warning and exhortation. He   248 who will not heed or believe this may go his own way until he learns it by experience. But it needs to be impressed upon the young people so that they may be on their guard and not follow the old, wayward crowd, but may keep their eyes fixed upon God's commandment, lest his wrath and punishment come upon them too. Our responsibility 249 is only to instruct and reprove by means of God's Word. To restrain open lawlessness is the responsibility of princes and magistrates. They should be alert and resolute enough to establish and maintain order in all areas of trade and commerce in order that the poor may not be burdened and oppressed and in order that they may not themselves be charged with other men's sins.

Enough has been said concerning the nature of stealing. It is 250 not to be confined to narrow limits but must extend to all our relations with our neighbors. To sum up, as we have done in the previous commandments: On one hand, we are forbidden to do our neighbor any injury or wrong in any way imaginable, whether by damaging, withholding, or interfering with his possessions and property. We are not even to consent to or permit such a thing, but are rather to avert and prevent it. On the other hand, we are 251 commanded to promote and further our neighbor's interests, and when he suffers want we are to help, share, and lend to both friends and foes.

Anyone who seeks and desires good works will here find 252 ample opportunity to do things which are heartily acceptable and pleasing to God. Moreover, he graciously lavishes upon them a wonderful blessing: We shall be richly rewarded for all the help and kindness we show to our neighbor, as King Solomon teaches in Prov. 19:17, "He who is kind to the poor lends to the Lord, and he will repay him for his deed." Here you have a rich Lord. 253 Surely he is sufficient for your needs and will let you lack or want for nothing. Thus with a happy conscience you can enjoy a hundred times more than you could scrape together by perfidy and injustice. Whoever does not desire this blessing will find wrath and misfortune enough.

THE EIGHTH COMMANDMENT

You shall not bear false
witness against your
neighbor.

What does this mean for us?

We are to fear and love God
so that we do not betray, slander,
    or lie about our neighbor,
but defend him, speak well of him,
and explain his actions in the kindest
    way.

THE EIGHTH COMMANDMENT

"You shall not bear false witness against your neighbor."   254

Besides our own body, our wife or husband, and our temporal   255
property, we have one more treasure which is indispensable to us,
namely, our honor and good name, for it is intolerable to live among
men in public disgrace and contempt. Therefore God will not   256
have our neighbor deprived of his reputation, honor, and character
any more than of his money and possessions; he would have every man
maintain his self-respect before his wife, children, servants, and
neighbors. In its first and simplest meaning, as the words stand   257
("You shall not bear false witness"), this commandment pertains to
public courts of justice, where a poor, innocent man is accused and
maligned by false witnesses and consequently punished in his body,
property, or honor.

This problem appears to concern us only a little at present, but   258
among the Jews it was extremely common. That nation had an
excellent, orderly government, and even now, where there is such a
government, instances of this sin still occur. The reason is this:
Where judges, mayors, princes, or others in authority sit in judgment,
we always find that, true to the usual course of the world, men are
loath to offend anyone. Instead, they speak dishonestly with an eye
to gaining favor, money, prospects, or friendship. Consequently, a
poor man is inevitably oppressed, loses his case, and suffers punish-

ment. It is the universal misfortune of the world that men of integrity seldom preside in courts of justice.

A judge ought, above all, to be a man of integrity, and not   259 only upright but also a wise, sagacious, brave, and fearless man. Likewise, a witness should be fearless; more than that, he should be an upright man. He who is to administer justice equitably in all cases will often offend good friends, relatives, neighbors, and the rich and powerful who are in a position to help or harm him. He must therefore be quite blind, shutting his eyes and ears to everything but the evidence presented, and make his decision accordingly.

The first application of this commandment, then, is that   260 everyone should help his neighbor maintain his rights. He must not allow these rights to be thwarted or distorted but should promote and resolutely guard them, whether he be judge or witness, let the consequences be what they may. Here we have a goal set for our   261 jurists: perfect justice and equity in every case. They should let right remain right, not perverting or conc   ing or suppressing anything on account of anyone's money, property, honor, or power. This is one aspect of the commandment, and its plainest meaning, applying to all that takes place in court.

Next, it extends much further when it is applied to spiritual   262 jurisdiction or administration. Here, too, everyone bears false witness against his neighbor. Wherever there are godly preachers and Christians, they must endure having the world call them heretics, apostates, even seditious and accursed scoundrels. Moreover, the Word of God must undergo the most shameful and spiteful persecution and blasphemy; it is contradicted, perverted, misused, and misinterpreted. But let this pass; it is the blind world's nature to condemn and persecute the truth and the children of God and yet consider this no sin.

The third aspect of this commandment concerns us all. It   263 forbids all sins of the tongue by which we may injure or offend our neighbor. False witness is clearly a work of the tongue. Whatever is done with the tongue against a neighbor, then, is forbidden by God. This applies to false preachers with their corrupt teaching and blasphemy, to false judges and witnesses with their corrupt behavior in court and their lying and malicious talk outside of court. It   264 applies particularly to the detestable, shameful vice of back-biting or slander by which the devil rides us. Of this much could be said. It is a common vice of human nature that everyone would rather hear evil than good about his neighbor. Evil though we are, we cannot tolerate having evil spoken of us; we want the golden compliments of the whole world. Yet we cannot bear to hear the best spoken of others.

To avoid this vice, therefore, we should note that nobody has   265 the right to judge and reprove his neighbor publicly, even when he has seen a sin committed, unless he has been authorized to judge and reprove. There is a great difference between judging sin and 266 having knowledge of sin. Knowledge of sin does not entail the right to judge it. I may see and hear that my neighbor sins, but to make him the talk of the town is not my business. If I interfere and pass sentence on him, I fall into a greater sin than his. When you become aware of a sin, simply make your ears a tomb and bury it until you are appointed a judge and authorized to administer punishment by virtue of your office.

Those are called backbiters who are not content just to know 267 but rush ahead and judge. Learning a bit of gossip about someone else, they spread it into every corner, relishing and delighting in it like pigs that roll in the mud and root around in it with their snouts. This 268 is nothing else than usurping the judgment and office of God, pronouncing the severest kind of verdict and sentence, or the harshest verdict a judge can pronounce is to declare somebody a thief, a murderer, a traitor, etc. Whoever therefore ventures to accuse his neighbor of such guilt assumes as much authority as the emperor and all magistrates. For though you do not wield the sword, you use your venomous tongue to the disgrace and harm of your neighbor.

Therefore God forbids you to speak evil about another even 269 though, to your certain knowledge, he is guilty. All the more urgent is the prohibition if you are not sure but have it only from hearsay. But you say: "Why shouldn't I speak if it is the truth?" I reply: 270 "Why don't you bring it before the regular judge?" "Oh, I cannot prove it publicly; I might be called a liar and sent away in disgrace." Ah, now do you smell the roast? If you do not trust yourself to make your charges before the proper authorities, then hold your tongue. Keep your knowledge to yourself and do not give it out to others. For when you repeat a story that you cannot prove, even if it is true, you appear as a liar. Besides, you act like a knave, for no man should be deprived of his honor and good name unless these have first been taken away from him publicly.

Every report, then, that cannot be adequately proved is false 271 witness. No one should publicly assert as truth what is not 272 publicly substantiated. In short, what is secret should be allowed to remain secret, or at any rate be reproved in secret, as we shall hear. Therefore, if you encounter somebody with a worthless tongue 273 who gossips and slanders someone, rebuke him straight to his face and make him blush for shame. Then you will silence many a one who otherwise would bring some poor man into disgrace, from which he could scarcely clear himself. For honor and good name are easily taken away, but not easily restored.

So you see that we are absolutely forbidden to speak evil of 274 our neighbor. Exception is made, however, of civil magistrates, preachers, and parents, for we must interpret this commandment in such a way that evil shall not go unpunished. We have seen that the Fifth Commandment forbids us to injure anyone physically, and yet an exception is made of the hangman. By virtue of his office he does not do his neighbor good but only harm and evil, yet he does not sin against God's commandment because God of his own accord instituted that office, and as he warns in the Fifth Commandment, he has reserved to himself the right of punishment. Likewise, although no one has in his own person the right to judge and condemn anyone, yet if they whose duty it is fail to do so, they sin as much as those who take the law into their own hands without such a commission. Necessity requires one to report evil, to prefer charges, to attest, 275 examine, and witness. It is no different from the situation of the physician who, to cure a patient, is sometimes compelled to examine and handle his private parts. Just so, magistrates, parents, even brothers and sisters and other good friends are under mutual obligation to reprove evil where it is necessary and beneficial.

But the right way to deal with this matter would be to observe 276 the order laid down by the Gospel, Matthew 19,[2] where Christ says, "If your brother sins against you, go and tell him his fault, between you and him alone." Here you have a fine, precious precept for governing the tongue which ought to be carefully noted if we are to avoid this detestable abuse. Let this be your rule, then, that you should not be quick to spread slander and gossip about your neighbor but admonish him privately so that he may amend. Likewise, if someone should whisper to you what this or that person has done, teach him, if he saw the wrongdoing, to go and reprove the man personally, otherwise to hold his tongue.

This lesson you can learn from the daily management of the 277 household. When the master of the house sees a servant failing to do his duty, he takes him to task personally. If he were so foolish as to leave the servant at home while he went out on the streets to complain to his neighbors, he would no doubt be told: "You fool! That is none of our business. Why don't you tell him yourself?" And that would be the brotherly thing to say, for the evil would 278 be corrected and the neighbor's honor maintained. As Christ himself says in the same passage, "If he listens to you, you have gained your brother." Then you have done a great and excellent work. Do you think it is an insignificant thing to gain a brother? Let all monks and holy orders step forth, with all their works heaped up together, and see if they can make the boast that they have gained one brother!

Christ teaches further: "If he does not listen, take one or two 279 others along with you, that every word may be confirmed by the

[2] Matt. 18:15. The reference was corrected in later editions.

evidence of two or three witnesses." [3] So the individual is to be dealt
with personally and not gossiped about behind his back. If this   280
does not help, then bring the matter before the public, either before
the civil or the ecclesiastical court. Then you do not stand alone.
You have witnesses with you through whom you can convict the guilty
one and on whose testimony the judge can base his decision and
sentence. This is the right procedure for restraining and reforming a
wicked person. But if you gossip about someone in every corner   281
and root around in the filth, nobody will be reformed. Moreover,
when you are called upon to witness, you will probably deny having
said anything. It would serve such gossips right to have their   282
sport spoiled, as a warning to others. If you were acting for   283
your neighbor's improvement or from love of the truth, you would not
sneak about in secret, shunning the light of day.

All this refers to secret sins. But where the sin is so public   284
that the judge and the whole world are aware of it, you can without
sin shun and avoid the person as one who has brought disgrace upon
himself, and you may testify publicly concerning him. For when an
affair is manifest to everybody there can be no question of slander or
injustice or false witness. For example, we now censure the pope and
his teaching, which is publicly set forth in books and shouted throughout the world. Where the sin is public, the punishment ought to be
public so that everyone may know how to guard against it.

Now we have the sum and substance of this commandment: 285
No one shall harm his neighbor, whether friend or foe, with his
tongue. No one shall speak evil of him, whether truly or falsely,
unless it is done with proper authority or for his improvement. A
person should use his tongue to speak only good of everyone, to cover
his neighbor's sins and infirmities, to overlook them, and to cloak and
veil them with his own honor. Our chief reason for doing so   286
should be the one which Christ indicates in the Gospel, and in which
he means to embrace all the commandments concerning our neighbor,
"Whatever you wish that men would do to you, do so to them." [4]

Even nature teaches the same thing in our own bodies, as   287
St. Paul says in I Cor. 12:22, 23, "The parts of the body which seem
to be weaker are indispensable, and those parts of the body which we
think less honorable we invest with the greater honor; and our
unpresentable parts are treated with greater modesty." No one covers
his face, eyes, nose, and mouth; we do not need to, for they are our
most honorable members. But the weakest members, of which we are
ashamed, we carefully conceal. Our hands and eyes, even the whole
body, must help to cover and veil them. Thus in our relations   288

[3] Matt. 18:16.
[4] Matt. 7:12.

with one another, we should veil whatever blemishes and infirmities we find in our neighbor, doing our utmost to serve and help him to promote his honor. On the other hand, we should prevent everything that tends to his disgrace. It is a particularly fine, noble virtue 289 always to put the best construction upon all we may hear about our neighbor, as long as it is not a notorious evil, and to defend him against the poisonous tongues of those who are busy wherever they can pry out and pounce on something to criticize in their neighbor, misconstruing and twisting things in the worst way. This is what happens now especially to the precious Word of God and its preachers.

This commandment, then, embraces a great multitude of good 290 works which please God most highly and bring abundant blessings, if only the blind world and the false saints would recognize them. There is nothing about a man or in a man that can do greater 291 good or greater harm, in spiritual or in temporal matters, than this smallest and weakest of his members, the tongue.[5]

[5] Cf. James 3:5.

THE NINTH COMMANDMENT

*You shall not covet your
neighbor's house.*

What does this mean for us?

> We are to fear and love God
> so that we do not desire to get our
>   neighbor's possessions by scheming,
> or by pretending to have a right to them,
> but always help him keep what is his.

THE TENTH COMMANDMENT

*You shall not covet your
neighbor's wife, or his
manservant, or his maid-
servant, or his cattle,
or anything that is your
neighbor's.*

What does this mean for us?

> We are to fear and love God
> so that we do not tempt or coax away
>   from our neighbor his wife or his
>   workers,
> but encourage them to remain loyal.

THE NINTH AND TENTH COMMANDMENTS

"You shall not covet your neighbor's house."   292
*"You shall not covet his wife, man-servant, maid-servant, cattle, or
anything that is his."*

These two commandments, taken literally, were given exclu- 293
sively to the Jews; nevertheless, in part they also apply to us. The
Jews did not interpret them as referring to unchastity or theft, since
these vices were sufficiently forbidden in commandments above. They

thought they were keeping the commandments when they obeyed the injunctions and prohibitions contained in them. God therefore added these two commandments to teach them that it is sinful and forbidden to covet our neighbor's wife or property, or to have any designs upon them. Especially were these commandments needed 294 because under the Jewish government man-servants and maid-servants were not free, as now, to serve for wages according to their own choice; with their body and all they had they were their master's property, the same as his cattle and other possessions. Moreover, 295 every man had power to dismiss his wife publicly by giving her a bill of divorce[6] and to take another wife. So there was a danger among them that if anyone took a fancy to another's wife, he might on any flimsy excuse dismiss his own wife and estrange the other's from him so that he might legally take her. They considered this no more a sin or disgrace than it is now for a master to dismiss his servants or entice his neighbor's from him.

Therefore, I say, they interpreted these commandments 296 correctly (though they also have a broader and higher application) to forbid anyone, even with a specious pretext, to covet or scheme to despoil his neighbor of what belongs to him, such as his wife, servants, house, fields, meadows, or cattle. Above, the seventh commandment prohibits seizing or withholding another's possessions to which you have no right. But here it is also forbidden to entice anything away from your neighbor, even though in the eyes of the world you could do it honorably, without accusation or blame for fraudulent dealing.

Such is nature that we all begrudge another's having as much 297 as we have. Everyone acquires all he can and lets others look out for themselves. Yet we all pretend to be upright. We know how to 298 put up a fine front to conceal our rascality. We think up artful dodges and sly tricks (better and better ones are being devised daily) under the guise of justice. We brazenly dare to boast of it, and insist that it should be called not rascality but shrewdness and business acumen. In this we are abetted by jurists and lawyers who twist and stretch 299 the law to suit their purpose, straining words and using them for pretexts, without regard for equity or for our neighbor's plight. In short, whoever is sharpest and shrewdest in such affairs gets most advantage out of the law, for as the saying has it, "The law favors the vigilant."

This last commandment, then, is addressed not to those whom 300 the world considers wicked rogues, but precisely to the most upright— to people who wish to be commended as honest and virtuous because they have not offended against the preceding commandments. To this class the Jews especially claimed to belong, as many great nobles, lords, and princes do now. For the common masses belong much

[6] Cf. Deut. 24:1.

farther down in the scale, where the Seventh Commandment applies, since they are not much concerned about questions of honor and right when it comes to acquiring possessions.

This situation occurs most frequently in lawsuits in which   301 someone sets out to gain and squeeze something out of his neighbor. For example, when people wrangle and wrestle over a large inheritance, real estate, etc., they resort to whatever arguments have the least semblance of right, so varnishing and garnishing them that the law supports them, and they gain such secure title to the property as to put it beyond complaint or dispute. Similarly, if anyone covets   302 a castle, city, county, or other great estate, he practices bribery, through friendly connections and by any other means at his disposal, until the property is taken away from the owner and legally awarded to him with letters patent and the seal of the prince attesting that it was acquired lawfully.

The same thing happens in ordinary business affairs, where one   303 cunningly slips something out of another's hand so that the victim is helpless to prevent it. Or, seeing an opportunity for profit—let us say, when a man because of adversity or debt cannot hold on to his property, nor yet sell it without loss—he hurries and worries him until he acquires a half or more of it; and yet this must not be considered as illegally acquired, but rather as honestly purchased. Hence the sayings, "First come, first served," and "Every man must look out for himself while others shift for themselves." Who is ingenious   304 enough to imagine how much he can acquire by such specious pretexts? The world does not consider this wrong, and it does not see that the neighbor is being taken advantage of and forced to sacrifice what he cannot spare without injury. Yet no one wishes this to happen to himself. From this it is clear that all these pretexts and shams are false.

This was also the case in ancient times with respect to wives.   305 They knew tricks like this: If a man took a fancy to another woman, he managed, either personally or through others and by any of a number of ways, to make her husband displeased with her, or she became so disobedient and hard to live with that her husband was obliged to dismiss her and leave her to the other man. That sort of thing undoubtedly was quite prevalent in the time of the law, for we read even in the Gospel[7] that King Herod took his brother's wife while the latter was still living, and yet posed as an honorable, upright man, as St. Mark testifies. Such examples, I trust, will not be   306 found among us, except that someone may by trickery entice a rich bride away from another, for in the New Testament[8] married people are forbidden to be divorced. But it is not uncommon among us for

[7] Matt. 14:3f.; Mark 6:17ff.
[8] Matt. 5:31f., 19:3-9; Mark 10:2-12; Luke 16:18; I Cor. 7:10f.

a person to lure away another's man-servant or maid-servant or otherwise estrange them with fair words.

However these things may be, you must learn that God does 307 not wish you to deprive your neighbor of anything that is his, letting him suffer loss while you gratify your greed, even though in the eyes of the world you might honorably retain the property. To do so is dark and underhanded wickedness, and, as we say, it is all done "under the hat" [9] so as to escape detection. Although you may act as if you have wronged no one, you have trespassed on your neighbor's rights. It may not be called stealing or fraud, yet it is coveting—that is, having designs upon your neighbor's property, luring it away from him against his will, and begrudging what God gave him. The 308 judge and the public may have to leave you in possession of it, but God will not, for he sees your wicked heart and the deceitfulness of the world. If you give the world an inch, it will take a yard, and at length open injustice and violence follow.

Let these commandments therefore retain their general appli- 309 cation. We are commanded not to desire harm to our neighbor, nor become accessory to it, nor give occasion for it; we are willingly to leave him what is his, and promote and protect whatever may be profitable and serviceable to him, as we wish that he would do to us. Thus these commandments are directed especially against envy 310 and miserable covetousness, God's purpose being to destroy all the roots and causes of our injuries to our neighbors. Therefore he sets it forth in plain words: "You shall not covet," etc. Above all, he wants our hearts to be pure, even though as long as we live here we cannot reach that ideal. So this commandment remains, like all the rest, one that constantly accuses us and shows just how upright we really are in God's sight.

[9] An expression derived from sorcery.

WHAT DOES GOD SAY OF ALL THESE
COMMANDMENTS?

He says:

*"I, the Lord your God, am a jealous
    God,*

*visiting the iniquity of the fathers
    upon the children to the third
    and fourth generation of those
    who hate me,*

*but showing steadfast love to
    thousands of those who love me
and keep my commandments."*

What does this mean for us?

God warns that he will punish all
    who break these commandments.
Therefore we are to fear his wrath
    and not disobey him.
But he promises grace and every
    blessing to all who keep these
    commandments.
Therefore we are to love and trust him,
    and gladly do what he commands.

CONCLUSION OF THE TEN COMMANDMENTS[1]

Here, then, we have the Ten Commandments, a summary of   3 1 1
divine teaching on what we are to do to make our whole life pleasing
to God. They are the true fountain from which all good works must
spring, the true channel through which all good works must flow.
Apart from these Ten Commandments no deed, no conduct can be
good or pleasing to God, no matter how great or precious it may be in
the eyes of the world.

Let us see, now, how our great saints can boast of their   3 1 2
spiritual orders and the great, difficult works which they have fashioned

[1] This title was inserted later.

while they neglect these commandments as if they were too insignificant or had been fulfilled long ago.

It seems to me that we shall have our hands full to keep these 313 commandments, practicing gentleness, patience, love toward enemies, chastity, kindness, etc., and all that these virtues involve. But such works are not important or impressive in the eyes of the world. They are not unusual and pompous, restricted to special times, places, rites, and ceremonies, but are common, everyday domestic duties of one neighbor toward another, with no show about them. On the other 314 hand, those other works captivate all eyes and ears. Aided by great pomp, splendor, and magnificent buildings, they are so adorned that everything gleams and glitters. There is burning of incense, singing and ringing of bells, lighting of tapers and candles until nothing else can be seen or heard. For when a priest stands in a gold-embroidered chasuble[2] or a layman remains on his knees a whole day in church, this is considered a precious work that cannot be sufficiently extolled. But when a poor girl tends a little child, or faithfully does what she is told, that is regarded as nothing. Otherwise, why should monks and nuns go into cloisters?

Just think, is it not a devilish presumption on the part of those 315 desperate saints to dare to find a higher and better way of life than the Ten Commandments teach? They pretend, as we have said, that this is a simple life for the ordinary man, whereas theirs is for the saints and the perfect. They fail to see, these miserable, blind 316 people, that no man can achieve so much as to keep one of the Ten Commandments as it ought to be kept. Both the Creed and the Lord's Prayer must help us, as we shall hear. Through them we must seek and pray for help and receive it continually. Therefore all their boasting amounts to as much as if I boasted, "Of course, I haven't a single groschen to pay, but I promise to pay ten gulden." [3]

All this I say and repeat in order that men may get rid of the 317 pernicious abuse which has become so deeply rooted and still clings to every man, and that all classes of men on earth may accustom themselves to look only to these precepts and heed them. It will be a long time before men produce a doctrine or social order equal to that of the Ten Commandments, for they are beyond human power to fulfill. Anyone who does fulfill them is a heavenly, angelic man, far above all holiness on earth. Just concentrate upon them and 318 test yourself thoroughly, do your very best, and you will surely find so much to do that you will neither seek nor pay attention to any other works or other kind of holiness.

[2] An elaborate vestment for the officiant at Mass. Cf. Smalcald Articles, Preface, 13.

[3] There were 21 groschen, small gold or silver coins (English: groat), to a gulden.

Let this suffice concerning the first part,[4] both for instruction   3 1 9
and for admonition. In conclusion, however, we must repeat the text
which we have already treated above in connection with the First
Commandment[5] in order to show how much effort God requires us to
devote to learning how to teach and practice the Ten Commandments.

"I the Lord, your God, am a jealous God, visiting the iniquity   3 2 0
of the fathers upon the children to the third and fourth generation of
them that hate me; but to those who love and keep my commandments,
I show mercy unto a thousand generations."

Although primarily attached to the First Commandment, as we   3 2 1
heard above, this appendix was intended to apply to all the commandments, and all of them as a whole ought to be referred and directed
to it. For this reason I said that we should keep it before the young
and insist that they learn and remember it so that we may see why we
are constrained and compelled to keep these Ten Commandments.
This appendix ought to be regarded as attached to each individual
commandment, penetrating and pervading them all.

Now, as we said before, these words contain both a wrathful   3 2 2
threat and a friendly promise, not only to terrify and warn us but also
to attract and allure us. These words, therefore, ought to be received
and esteemed as a serious matter to God because he himself here
declares how important the commandments are to him and how
strictly he will watch over them, fearfully and terribly punishing all
who despise and transgress his commandments; and again, how richly
he will reward, bless, and bestow all good things on those who prize
them and gladly act and live in accordance with them. Thus he   3 2 3
demands that all our actions proceed from a heart that fears and
regards God alone and, because of this fear, avoids all that is contrary
to his will, lest he be moved to wrath; and, conversely, trusts him alone
and for his sake does all that he asks of us, because he shows himself
a kind father and offers us every grace and blessing.

This is exactly the meaning and right interpretation of the   3 2 4
first and chief commandment, from which all the others proceed.
This word, "You shall have no other gods," means simply, "You shall
fear, love, and trust me as your one true God." Wherever a man's heart
has such an attitude toward God, he has fulfilled this commandment
and all the others. On the other hand, whoever fears and loves
anything else in heaven and on earth will keep neither this nor any
other. Thus the entire Scriptures have proclaimed and presented   3 2 5
this commandment everywhere, emphasizing these two things, fear of
God and trust in God. The prophet David particularly teaches it
throughout the Psalter, as when he says, "The Lord takes pleasure in
those who fear him, in those who hope in his mercy" (Ps. 147:11).

---

[4] I.e., the first part of the Catechism.
[5] Section 30, above.

He seems to explain the whole commandment in one verse, as if to say, "The Lord takes pleasure in those who have no other gods."

Thus the First Commandment is to illuminate and impart its 326 splendor to all the others. In order that this may be constantly repeated and never forgotten, therefore, you must let these concluding words run through all the commandments, like the clasp or the hoop of a wreath that binds the end to the beginning and holds everything together. For example, in the Second Commandment we are told to fear God and not take his name in vain by cursing, lying, deceiving, and other kinds of corruption and wickedness, but to use his name properly by calling upon him in prayer, praise, and thanksgiving, which spring from that love and trust which the First Commandment requires. Similarly, this fear, love, and trust should impel us not to despise his Word, but learn it, hear it gladly, keep it holy, and honor it.

So, through the following commandments which concern our 327 neighbor, everything proceeds from the force of the First Commandment: We are to honor father and mother, masters, and all in authority, being submissive and obedient to them not on their own account but for God's sake. For you dare not respect or fear father or mother wrongly, doing or omitting to do things simply in order to please them. Rather, ask what God wants of you and what he will quite surely demand of you. If you omit that, you have an angry judge; otherwise, you have a gracious father.

Again, you are to do your neighbor no harm, injury, or 328 violence, nor in any way molest him, either in his person, his wife, his property, his honor or rights, as these things are commanded in that order, even though you have the opportunity and occasion to do so and no man may reprove you. On the contrary, you should do good to all men, help them and promote their interests, however and whenever you can, purely out of love to God and in order to please him, in the confidence that he will abundantly reward you for all you do. Thus you see how the First Commandment is the chief 329 source and fountainhead from which all the others proceed; again, to it they all return and upon it they depend, so that end and beginning are all linked and bound together.

It is useful and necessary always to teach, admonish, and 330 remind young people of all this so that they may be brought up, not only with blows and compulsion, like cattle, but in the fear and reverence of God. These are not trifles of men but the commandments of the most high God, who watches over them with great earnestness, who vents his wrath upon those who despise them, and, on the contrary, abundantly rewards those who keep them. Where men consider this and take it to heart, there will arise a spontaneous impulse and desire gladly to do God's will. Therefore it is not without 331 reason that the Old Testament commands men to write the Ten

Commandments on every wall and corner, and even on their garments.[6] Not that we are to have them there merely for a display, as the Jews did,[7] but we are to keep them incessantly before our eyes and constantly in our memory, and practice them in all our works and ways. Everyone is to make them his daily habit in all 332 circumstances, in all his affairs and dealings, as if they were written everywhere he looks, and even wherever he goes or wherever he stands. Thus, both for himself at home, and abroad among his neighbors, he will find occasion enough to practice the Ten Commandments, and no one need search far for them.

From all this it is obvious once again how highly these Ten 333 Commandments are to be exalted and extolled above all orders, commands, and works which are taught and practiced apart from them. Here we can fling out the challenge: Let all wise men and saints step forward and produce, if they can, any work like that which God in these commandments so earnestly requires and enjoins under threat of his greatest wrath and punishment, while at the same time he adds such glorious promises that he will shower us with all good things and blessings. Therefore we should prize and value them above all other teachings as the greatest treasure God has given us.

[6] Deut. 6:8f., 11:20.
[7] Cf. Matt. 23:5.

SECOND PART: THE CREED

Thus far we have heard the first part of Christian doctrine. In it 1
we have seen all that God wishes us to do or not to do. The Creed
properly follows, setting forth all that we must expect and receive
from God; in brief, it teaches us to know him perfectly. It is given 2
in order to help us do what the Ten Commandments require of us.
For, as we said above, they are set on so high a plane that all human
ability is far too feeble and weak to keep them. Therefore it is as
necessary to learn this part as it is the other so that we may know
where and how to obtain strength for this task. If we could by our 3
own strength keep the Ten Commandments as they ought to be kept,
we would need neither the Creed nor the Lord's Prayer. But before 4
we explain the advantage and necessity of the Creed, it is sufficient, as
a first step, for very simple persons to learn to understand the Creed
itself.

In the first place, the Creed used to be divided into twelve 5
articles.[8] Of course, if all the thoughts contained in the Scriptures and
belonging to the Creed were gathered together, there would be many
more articles, nor could they all be clearly expressed in so few words.
But to make it most clear and simple for teaching to children, we 6
shall briefly sum up the entire Creed in three articles,[9] according to the
three persons of the Godhead, to whom all that we believe is related.
The first article, of God the Father, explains creation; the second, of
the Son, redemption; the third, of the Holy Spirit, sanctification.
Hence the Creed may be briefly comprised in these few words: "I 7
believe in God the Father, who created me; I believe in God the Son,
who redeemed me; I believe in the Holy Spirit, who sanctifies me."
One God and one faith, but three persons, and therefore three articles
or confessions. Let us briefly comment on these words. 8

[8] Tradition, dating to about A.D. 400, held that each of the twelve apostles
contributed one article to the Creed.
[9] Luther proposed the three-fold division in "A Brief Form of the Creed"
(1520), *WA*, 7:214.

THE FIRST ARTICLE
I believe in God the Father
almighty, Maker of heaven
and earth.

What does this mean?

I believe that God has created me
  and all that exists.
He has given me and still preserves
  my body and soul with all their
  powers.

He provides me with food and clothing,
  home and family, daily work, and all
  I need from day to day.
God also protects me in time of danger
  and guards me from every evil.

All this he does out of fatherly and
  divine goodness and mercy,
  though I do not deserve it.
Therefore I surely ought to thank and
  praise, serve and obey him.

This is most certainly true.

The First Article

"*I believe in God, the Father almighty, maker of heaven and* 9
earth."

These words give us a brief description of God the Father, his 10
nature, his will, and his work. Since the Ten Commandments have
explained that we are to have no more than one God, it may be asked:
"What kind of being is God? What does he do? How can we praise
or portray or describe him in such a way as to make him known?"
This is taught here and in the following articles. Thus the Creed is
nothing else than a response and confession of Christians based on the
First Commandment. If you were to ask a young child, "My boy, 11
what kind of God have you? What do you know about him?" he
could say, "First, my God is the Father, who made heaven and earth.
Apart from him alone I have no other God, for there is no one else
who could create heaven and earth."

For the somewhat more advanced and the educated, however, 12 all three articles can be treated more fully and divided into as many parts as there are words. But for young pupils it is enough to indicate the most necessary points, namely, as we have said, that this article deals with creation. We should emphasize the words, "maker of heaven and earth." What is meant by these words, "I believe in 13 God, the Father almighty, maker," etc.? Answer: I hold and believe that I am a creature of God; that is, that he has given and constantly sustains my body, soul, and life, my members great and small, all the faculties of my mind, my reason and understanding, and so forth; my food and drink, clothing, means of support, wife and child, servants, house and home, etc. Besides, he makes all creation help 14 provide the comforts and necessities of life—sun, moon, and stars in the heavens, day and night, air, fire, water, the earth and all that it brings forth, birds and fish, beasts, grain and all kinds of produce. Moreover, he gives all physical and temporal blessings—good 15 government, peace, security. Thus we learn from this article that 16 none of us has his life of himself, or anything else that has been mentioned here or can be mentioned, nor can he by himself preserve any of them, however small and unimportant. All this is comprehended in the word "Creator."

Moreover, we confess that God the Father not only has given 17 us all that we have and see before our eyes, but also daily guards and defends us against every evil and misfortune, warding off all sorts of danger and disaster. All this he does out of pure love and goodness, without our merit, as a kind father who cares for us so that no evil may befall us. But further discussion of this subject belongs in 18 the other two parts of this article, where we say, "Father almighty."

Hence, since everything we possess, and everything in heaven 19 and on earth besides, is daily given and sustained by God, it inevitably follows that we are in duty bound to love, praise, and thank him without ceasing, and, in short, to devote all these things to his service, as he has required and enjoined in the Ten Commandments.

Much could be said if we were to describe in detail how few 20 people believe this article. We all pass over it, hear it, and recite it, but we neither see nor consider what the words enjoin on us. For 21 if we believed it with our whole heart, we would also act accordingly, and not swagger about and brag and boast as if we had life, riches, power, honor, and such things of ourselves, as if we ourselves were to be feared and served. This is the way the wretched, perverse world acts, drowned in its blindness, misusing all the blessings and gifts of God solely for its own pride and greed, pleasure and enjoyment, and never once turning to God to thank him or acknowledge him as Lord and Creator.

Therefore, this article would humble and terrify us all if we 22 believed it. For we sin daily with eyes and ears, hands, body and soul, money and property, and with all that we have. This is especially true of those who even fight against the Word of God. Yet Christians have this advantage, that they acknowledge themselves in duty bound to serve and obey him for all these things.

For this reason we ought daily to study this article and impress   23 it upon our minds. Everything we see, and every blessing that comes our way, should remind us of it. When we escape distress or danger, we should recognize that this is God's doing. He gives us all these things so that we may sense and see in them his fatherly heart and his boundless love toward us. Thus our hearts will be warmed and kindled with gratitude to God and a desire to use all these blessings to his glory and praise.

Such, very briefly, is the meaning of this article. It is all that   24 ordinary people need to learn at first, both about what we have and receive from God and about what we owe him in return. This is an excellent knowledge, but an even greater treasure. For here we see how the Father has given himself to us, with all his creatures, has abundantly provided for us in this life, and, further, has showered us with inexpressible eternal treasures through his Son and the Holy Spirit, as we shall hear.

THE SECOND ARTICLE
And in Jesus Christ
his only Son, our Lord;
who was conceived by the Holy
  Ghost,
born of the Virgin Mary;
suffered under Pontius Pilate,
  was crucified, dead, and buried;
he descended into hell;
the third day he rose again from
  the dead;
he ascended into heaven,
and sitteth on the right hand of
  God the Father almighty;
from thence he shall come
  to judge the quick and the dead.

What does this mean?
  I believe that Jesus Christ—
  true God, Son of the Father from
    eternity,
  and true man, born of the Virgin Mary—
  is my Lord.
  At great cost
  he has saved and redeemed me,
  a lost and condemned person.
  He has freed me
  from sin, death, and the power of the
    devil—
  not with silver or gold,
  but with his holy and precious blood
  and his innocent suffering and death.
  All this he has done that I may be his
    own,
  live under him in his kingdom,
  and serve him in everlasting righteous-
    ness, innocence, and blessedness,
  just as he is risen from the dead and
    lives and rules eternally.
  This is most certainly true.

118 CREED

THE SECOND ARTICLE

"And in Jesus Christ, his only Son, our Lord: who was conceived 25
by the Holy Spirit, born of the virgin Mary, suffered under Pontius
Pilate, was crucified, dead, and buried: he descended into hell, the
third day he rose from the dead, he ascended into heaven, and is seated
on the right hand of God, the Father almighty, whence he shall come
to judge the living and the dead."

Here we learn to know the second person of the Godhead, and 26
we see what we receive from God over and above the temporal goods
mentioned above—that is, how he has completely given himself to us,
withholding nothing. This article is very rich and far-reaching, but in
order to treat it briefly and simply, we shall take up one phrase which
contains the substance of the article; from it we shall learn how we
are redeemed. We shall concentrate on these words, "in Jesus Christ,
our Lord."

If you are asked, "What do you believe in the Second Article, 27
concerning Jesus Christ?" answer briefly, "I believe that Jesus Christ,
true Son of God, has become my Lord." What is it to "become a
Lord"? It means that he has redeemed me from sin, from the devil,
from death, and from all evil. Before this I had no Lord and King
but was captive under the power of the devil. I was condemned to
death and entangled in sin and blindness.

When we were created by God the Father, and had received 28
from him all kinds of good things, the devil came and led us into
disobedience, sin, death, and all evil. We lay under God's wrath and
displeasure, doomed to eternal damnation, as we had deserved.
There was no counsel, no help, no comfort for us until this only 29
and eternal Son of God, in his unfathomable goodness, had mercy on
our misery and wretchedness and came from heaven to help us.
Those tyrants and jailers now have been routed, and their place 30
has been taken by Jesus Christ, the Lord of life and righteousness and
every good and blessing. He has snatched us, poor lost creatures, from
the jaws of hell, won us, made us free, and restored us to the Father's
favor and grace. He has taken us as his own, under his protection, in
order that he may rule us by his righteousness, wisdom, power, life,
and blessedness.

Let this be the summary of this article, that the little word 31
"Lord" simply means the same as Redeemer, that is, he who has
brought us back from the devil to God, from death to life, from sin to
righteousness, and now keeps us safe there. The remaining parts of
this article simply serve to clarify and express how and by what means
this redemption was accomplished—that is, how much it cost Christ
and what he paid and risked in order to win us and bring us under his
dominion. That is to say, he became man, conceived and born without
sin, of the Holy Spirit and the Virgin, that he might become Lord

over sin; moreover, he suffered, died, and was buried that he might make satisfaction for me and pay what I owed, not with silver and gold but with his own precious blood. All this in order to become my Lord. For he did none of these things for himself, nor had he any need of them. Afterward he rose again from the dead, swallowed up[1] and devoured death, and finally ascended into heaven and assumed dominion at the right hand of the Father. The devil and all powers, therefore, must be subject to him and lie beneath his feet until finally, at the last day, he will completely divide and separate us from the wicked world, the devil, death, sin, etc.

But the proper place to explain all these different points is not   32 the brief children's sermons, but rather the longer sermons throughout the year, especially at the times appointed[2] for dealing at length with such articles as the birth, passion, resurrection, and ascension of Christ.

Indeed, the entire Gospel that we preach depends on the proper   33 understanding of this article. Upon it all our salvation and blessedness are based, and it is so rich and broad that we can never learn it fully.

[1] Cf. Isa. 25:8.
[2] Christmas, Lent, Easter, Ascension.

THE THIRD ARTICLE

I believe in the Holy Ghost;
the holy Christian church, the
  communion of saints;
the forgiveness of sins;
the resurrection of the body;
and the life everlasting. Amen.

What does this mean?

I believe that I cannot by my own
  understanding or effort
believe in Jesus Christ my Lord,
  or come to him.
But the Holy Spirit has called me
  through the Gospel,
enlightened me with his gifts,
and sanctified and kept me in true faith.

In the same way he calls, gathers,
  enlightens, and sanctifies
the whole Christian church on earth,
and keeps it united with Jesus Christ
  in the one true faith.

In this Christian church day after day
he fully forgives my sins
and the sins of all believers.
On the last day he will raise me and all
  the dead
and give me and all believers in Christ
  eternal life.

This is most certainly true.

The Third Article

"I believe in the Holy Spirit, the holy Christian church, the 34
communion of saints, the forgiveness of sins, the resurrection of the
body, and the life everlasting. Amen."

To this article, as I have said, I cannot give a better title than 35
"Sanctification." In it is expressed and portrayed the Holy Spirit and
his office, which is that he makes us holy. Therefore, we must
concentrate on the term "Holy Spirit," because it is so precise that we
can find no substitute for it. Many other kinds of spirits are 36
mentioned in the Scriptures, such as the spirit of man,[3] heavenly
spirits,[4] and the evil spirit.[5] But God's Spirit alone is called Holy Spirit,
that is, he who has sanctified and still sanctifies us. As the Father is
called Creator and the Son is called Redeemer, so on account of his
work the Holy Spirit must be called Sanctifier, the One who makes
holy. How does this sanctifying take place? Answer: Just as the 37
Son obtains dominion by purchasing us through his birth, death, and
resurrection, etc., so the Holy Spirit effects our sanctification through
the following: the communion of saints or Christian church, the
forgiveness of sins, the resurrection of the body, and the life everlasting. In other words, he first leads us into his holy community,
placing us upon the bosom of the church, where he preaches to us
and brings us to Christ.

Neither you nor I could ever know anything of Christ, or believe 38
in him and take him as our Lord, unless these were first offered to
us and bestowed on our hearts through the preaching of the Gospel
by the Holy Spirit. The work is finished and completed, Christ has
acquired and won the treasure for us by his sufferings, death, and
resurrection, etc. But if the work remained hidden and no one knew
of it, it would have been all in vain, all lost. In order that this
treasure might not be buried but put to use and enjoyed, God has
caused the Word to be published and proclaimed, in which he has given
the Holy Spirit to offer and apply to us this treasure of salvation.
Therefore to sanctify is nothing else than to bring us to the Lord 39
Christ to receive this blessing, which we could not obtain by ourselves.

Learn this article, then, as clearly as possible. If you are asked, 40
What do you mean by the words, "I believe in the Holy Spirit"? you
can answer, "I believe that the Holy Spirit makes me holy, as his name
implies." How does he do this? By what means? Answer: 41
"Through the Christian church, the forgiveness of sins, the resurrection
of the body, and the life everlasting." In the first place, he has a 42
unique community in the world. It is the mother that begets and bears

---

[3] E.g., I Cor. 2:11.

[4] Cf. II Macc. 11:6, 15:23. Luther interpreted these as the good angels.

[5] Cf. I Sam. 16:14, 23; Tobit 3:8; Acts 19:12, 15.

122

CREED

every Christian through the Word of God. The Holy Spirit reveals and preaches that Word, and by it he illumines and kindles hearts so that they grasp and accept it, cling to it, and persevere in it.

Where he does not cause the Word to be preached and does not 43 awaken understanding in the heart, all is lost. This was the case under the papacy, where faith was entirely shoved under the bench and no one recognized Christ as the Lord, or the Holy Spirit as the Sanctifier. That is, no one believed that Christ is our Lord in the sense that he won for us this treasure without our works and merits and made us acceptable to the Father. What was lacking here? There was no 44 Holy Spirit present to reveal this truth and have it preached. Men and evil spirits there were, teaching us to obtain grace and be saved by our works. Therefore there was no Christian church. For where 45 Christ is not preached, there is no Holy Spirit to create, call, and gather the Christian church, and outside it no one can come to the Lord Christ. Let this suffice concerning the substance of this 46 article. But since various points in it are not quite clear to the common people, we shall run through them also.

The Creed calls the holy Christian church a *communio sanc-* 47 *torum,* "a communion of saints." Both expressions have the same meaning. In early times the latter phrase was missing,[6] and it is unintelligible in our translation. If it is to be rendered idiomatically, we must express it quite differently. The word *ecclesia* properly means an assembly. We, however, are accustomed to the term 48 *Kirche,* "church," by which simple folk understand not a group of people but a consecrated house or building. But the house should not be called a church except for the single reason that the group of people assembles there. For we who assemble select a special place and give the house its name by virtue of the assembly. Thus the word "church" (*Kirche*) really means nothing else than a common assembly; it is not of German but of Greek origin, like the word *ecclesia.* In that language the word is *kyria,* and in Latin *curia.*[7] In our mother tongue therefore it ought to be called "a Christian congregation or assembly,"[8] or best and most clearly of all, "a holy Christian people."[9]

[6] In 1519 Luther expressed the opinion that the expression "communion of saints" was a late addition to the Creed, in apposition to "holy catholic Church" (*WA,* 2:190). The earliest extant version of the Creed containing the phrase is that attributed to Bishop Nicetas of Remesiana (*ca.* 400?).

[7] Luther was mistaken. *Kirche* comes not from the Greek *kyria* or *kyriake* but from the Celtic word *kyrk* (the circumscribed), related to the Latin *circus* and *carcer.* Again, curia is related not to the Greek *kyria* but to *Quiris* (Roman citizen).

[8] *Eine christliche Gemeine oder Sammlung.* In the Bible Luther always translated *ekklesia* with *Gemeine* (cf. Matt. 16:18; Acts 19:39f.; I Cor. 1:2; Gal. 1:2).

[9] *Eine heilige Christenheit.* In the treatise, "On the Councils and the Church" (1539), Luther urged substitution of *Christenheit* or *christliches Volk* for the "un-German" and "blind" word *Kirche. WA,* 50:624f.

Likewise the word *communio*, which is appended, should not be   49
translated "communion" but "community." [1] It is nothing but a
comment or interpretation by which someone wished to explain what
the Christian church is. But some among us, who understand neither
Latin nor German, have rendered this "communion of saints," although
no German would use or understand such an expression. To speak
idiomatically, we ought to say "a community of saints," that is, a
community composed only of saints, or, still more clearly, "a holy
community." This I say in order that the expression may be   50
understood; it has become so established in usage that it cannot well
be uprooted, and it would be next to heresy to alter a word.

This is the sum and substance of this phrase: I believe that   51
there is on earth a little holy flock or community of pure saints under
one head, Christ. It is called together by the Holy Spirit in one faith,
mind, and understanding. It possesses a variety of gifts, yet is united
in love without sect or schism. Of this community I also am a   52
part and member, a participant and co-partner[2] in all the blessings it
possesses. I was brought to it by the Holy Spirit and incorporated into
it through the fact that I have heard and still hear God's Word, which
is the first step in entering it. Before we had advanced this far, we
were entirely of the devil, knowing nothing of God and of Christ.
Until the last day the Holy Spirit remains with the holy community   53
or Christian people. Through it he gathers us, using it to teach and
preach the Word. By it he creates and increases sanctification, causing
it daily to grow and become strong in the faith and in the fruits of the
Spirit.

Further we believe that in this Christian church we have the   54
forgiveness of sins, which is granted through the holy sacraments and
absolution as well as through all the comforting words of the entire
Gospel. Toward forgiveness is directed everything that is to be
preached concerning the sacraments and, in short, the entire Gospel
and all the duties of Christianity. Forgiveness is needed constantly,
for although God's grace has been won by Christ, and holiness has
been wrought by the Holy Spirit through God's Word in the unity of
the Christian church, yet because we are encumbered with our flesh
we are never without sin.

Therefore everything in the Christian church is so ordered that   55
we may daily obtain full forgiveness of sins through the Word and
through signs[3] appointed to comfort and revive our consciences as
long as we live. Although we have sin, the Holy Spirit sees to it that
it does not harm us because we are in the Christian church, where there

---

[1] Not *Gemeinschaft* but *Gemeine.*
[2] Cf. I Cor. 1:9.
[3] The sacraments.

is full forgiveness of sin. God forgives us, and we forgive, bear with, and aid one another.

But outside the Christian church (that is, where the Gospel is 56 not) there is no forgiveness, and hence no holiness. Therefore, all who seek to merit holiness through their works rather than through the Gospel and the forgiveness of sin have expelled and separated themselves from the church.

Meanwhile, since holiness has begun and is growing daily, we 57 await the time when our flesh will be put to death, will be buried with all its uncleanness, and will come forth gloriously and arise to complete and perfect holiness in a new, eternal life. Now we are 58 only halfway pure and holy. The Holy Spirit must continue to work in us through the Word, daily granting forgiveness until we attain to that life where there will be no more forgiveness. In that life are only perfectly pure and holy people, full of goodness and righteousness, completely freed from sin, death, and all evil, living in new, immortal, and glorified bodies.

All this, then, is the office and work of the Holy Spirit, to 59 begin and daily to increase holiness on earth through these two means, the Christian church and the forgiveness of sins. Then, when we pass from this life, he will instantly perfect our holiness and will eternally preserve us in it by means of the last two parts of this article.

The term "resurrection of the flesh," however, is not well 60 chosen. When we Germans hear the word *Fleisch* (flesh), we think no farther than the butcher shop. Idiomatically we would say "resurrection of the body." [4] However, this is not of great importance, as long as the words are rightly understood.

This, then, is the article which must always remain in force. 61 Creation is past and redemption is accomplished, but the Holy Spirit carries on his work unceasingly until the last day. For this purpose he has appointed a community on earth, through which he speaks and does all his work. For he has not yet gathered together all his 62 Christian people, nor has he completed the granting of forgiveness. Therefore we believe in him who daily brings us into this community through the Word, and imparts, increases, and strengthens faith through the same Word and the forgiveness of sins. Then when his

[4] *Auferstehung des Leibs oder Leichnams.* In the early church, the word *sarkos* (flesh) apparently was inserted deliberately to combat the Gnostic tendency to assert that only the "spirit" was capable of being saved, that the body or flesh was by nature evil. In his exposition of John 1:14 (*WA*, 10¹: 235) Luther wrote: "By 'flesh' we should understand the whole human nature, body and soul, in the manner of the Scriptures, which call man 'flesh,' . . . and in the Creed we say, 'I believe in the resurrection of the flesh,' i.e., 'of all men.'" Older English translations of the Creed also read "resurrection of the flesh" until 1543, when in "The Necessary Doctrine and Erudition for any Christian Man," issued by Henry VIII, "resurrection of the body" was introduced.

work has been finished and we abide in it, having died to the world and all evil, he will finally make us perfectly and eternally holy. We now wait in faith for this to be accomplished through the Word.

Here in the Creed you have the entire essence of God, his will, 63 and his work exquisitely depicted in very short but rich words. In them consists all our wisdom, which surpasses all the wisdom, understanding, and reason of men. Although the whole world has sought painstakingly to learn what God is and what he thinks and does, yet it has never succeeded in the least. But here you have everything in richest measure. In these three articles God himself has revealed 64 and opened to us the most profound depths of his fatherly heart, his sheer, unutterable love. He created us for this very purpose, to redeem and sanctify us. Moreover, having bestowed upon us everything in heaven and on earth, he has given us his Son and his Holy Spirit, through whom he brings us to himself. As we explained before, 65 we could never come to recognize the Father's favor and grace were it not for the Lord Christ, who is a mirror of the Father's heart. Apart from him we see nothing but an angry and terrible Judge. But neither could we know anything of Christ, had it not been revealed by the Holy Spirit.

These articles of the Creed, therefore, divide and distinguish us 66 Christians from all other people on earth. All who are outside the Christian church, whether heathen, Turks, Jews, or false Christians and hypocrites, even though they believe in and worship only the one, true God, nevertheless do not know what his attitude is toward them. They cannot be confident of his love and blessing. Therefore they remain in eternal wrath and damnation, for they do not have the Lord Christ, and, besides, they are not illuminated and blessed by the gifts of the Holy Spirit.

Now you see that the Creed is a very different teaching from 67 the Ten Commandments. The latter teach us what we ought to do; the Creed tells what God does for us and gives to us. The Ten Commandments, moreover, are inscribed in the hearts of all men.[5] No human wisdom can comprehend the Creed; it must be taught by the Holy Spirit alone. Therefore the Ten Commandments do not 68 by themselves make us Christians, for God's wrath and displeasure still remain on us because we cannot fulfill his demands. But the Creed brings pure grace and makes us upright and pleasing to God. Through this knowledge we come to love and delight in all the 69 commandments of God because we see that God gives himself completely to us, with all his gifts and his power, to help us keep the Ten Commandments: the Father gives us all creation, Christ all his works, the Holy Spirit all his gifts.

[5] Cf. Rom. 2:15. Luther was thinking of the natural law. See also above, Third Commandment, 82 and footnote.

For the present this is enough concerning the Creed to lay a   70
foundation for the common people without overburdening them.
After they understand the substance of it, they may on their own
initiative learn more, relating to these teachings of the Catechism all
that they learn in the Scriptures, and thus advance and grow richer
in understanding. For as long as we live we shall have enough to
preach and learn on the subject of faith.

THIRD PART: THE LORD'S PRAYER

We have heard what we are to do and believe. The best and most   1
blessed life consists of these things. Now follows the third part, how
we are to pray. Mankind is in such a situation that no one can   2
keep the Ten Commandments perfectly, even though he has begun to
believe. Besides, the devil, along with the world and our flesh, resists
our efforts with all his power. Consequently nothing is so necessary as
to call upon God incessantly and drum into his ears our prayer that
he may give, preserve, and increase in us faith and obedience to the
Ten Commandments and remove all that stands in our way and hinders
us from fulfilling them. That we may know what and how to pray,   3
our Lord Christ himself has taught us both the way and the words, as
we shall see.

Before we explain the Lord's Prayer part by part, it is very   4
necessary to exhort and draw the people to prayer, as Christ and the
apostles also did.[6] The first thing to know is this: It is our duty to   5
pray because God has commanded it. We were told in the Second
Commandment, "You shall not take God's name in vain." Thereby
we are required to praise the holy name and pray or call upon it in
every need. For to call upon it is nothing else than to pray. Prayer,   6
therefore, is as strictly and solemnly commanded as all the other
commandments, such as having no other God, not killing, not stealing,
etc. Let no one think that it makes no difference whether I pray or
not, as vulgar people do who say in their delusion: "Why should I
pray? Who knows whether God heeds my prayer or cares to hear it?
If I do not pray, someone else will." Thus they fall into the habit of
never praying, alleging that since we reject false and hypocritical
prayers we teach that there is no duty or need to pray.

It is quite true that the kind of babbling and bellowing that used   7
to pass for prayers in the church was not really prayer. Such external
repetition, when properly used, may serve as an exercise for young
children, pupils, and simple folk; while it may be called singing or
reading exercise, it is not real prayer. To pray, as the Second   8
Commandment teaches, is to call upon God in every need. This God
requires of us; he has not left it to our choice. It is our duty and
obligation to pray if we want to be Christians, just as it is our duty and
obligation to obey our fathers and mothers and the civil authorities.
By invocation and prayer the name of God is glorified and used to
good purpose. This you should note above all, so that you may silence
and repel any thoughts that would prevent or deter us from praying.
It would be improper for a son to say to his father: "What is the use   9

---

[6] Cf. Matt. 7:7; Luke 18:1, 21:36; Rom. 12:12; Col. 4:2; I Thess. 5:17;
I Tim. 2:1; James 1:6, 5:13; I Pet. 4:8; Jude 20.

of being obedient? I will go and do as I please; what difference does it make?" But there stands the commandment, "You shall and must obey!" Just so, it is not left to my choice here whether to pray or not, but it is my duty and obligation [on pain of God's wrath and displeasure].[7]

[This should be kept in mind above all things so that you may 10 silence and repel thoughts which would prevent or deter us from praying, as though it made no great difference if we do not pray, or as though prayer were commanded for those who are holier and in better favor with God than we are. Indeed, the human heart is by nature so desperately wicked that it always flees from God, thinking that he neither wants nor cares for our prayers because we are sinners and have merited nothing but wrath. Against such thoughts, I say, we 11 should respect this commandment and turn to God so that we may not provoke his anger by such disobedience. By this commandment he makes it clear that he will not cast us out or drive us away, even though we are sinners; he wishes rather to draw us to himself so that we may humble ourselves before him, lament our misery and plight, and pray for grace and help. Therefore we read in the Scriptures that he is angry because those who were struck down for their sin did not return to him and assuage his wrath and seek grace by their prayers.]

From the fact that prayer is so urgently commanded, we ought 12 to conclude that we should by no means despise our prayers, but rather prize them highly. Take an illustration from the other commandments. A child should never despise obedience to his father 13 and mother, but should always reflect: "This is a work of obedience, and what I do has no other purpose than that it befits obedience and the commandment of God. On this I can rely and depend, and I can revere it highly, not because of my worthiness, but because of the commandment." So, too, here. What we shall pray, and for what, we should regard as demanded by God and done in obedience to him. We should think, "On my account this prayer would amount to nothing; but it is important because God has commanded it." So, no matter what he has to pray for, everybody should always approach God in obedience to this commandment.

We therefore urgently beg and exhort everyone to take these 14 words to heart and in no case to despise prayer. Prayer used to be taught, in the devil's name, in such a way that no one paid any attention to it, and men supposed it was enough if the act was performed, whether God heard it or not. But that is to stake prayer on luck and to mumble aimlessly. Such a prayer is worthless.

[7] The text in square brackets here and in the following paragraph (sections 10, 11) does not appear in the first edition of the Large Catechism, in the Jena edition of Luther's works, or in the 1580 German edition of the Book of Concord. It is found in revised editions of the Catechism (1529 and later), in the Latin translation of 1544, and freshly translated in the Latin Book of Concord, 1584.

We allow ourselves to be hindered and deterred by such 15 thoughts as these: "I am not holy enough or worthy enough; if I were as godly and holy as St. Peter or St. Paul, then I would pray." Away with such thoughts! The very commandment that applied to St. Paul applies also to me. The Second Commandment is given just as much on my account as on his. He can boast of no better or holier commandment than I.

Therefore you should say: "The prayer I offer is just as 16 precious, holy, and pleasing to God as those of St. Paul and the holiest of saints. The reason is this: I freely admit that he is holier in respect to his person, but not on account of the commandment. God does not regard prayer on account of the person, but on account of his Word and the obedience accorded it. On this commandment, on which all the saints base their prayer, I, too, base mine. Moreover, I pray for the same thing for which they all pray, or ever have prayed." [8]

This is the first and most important point, that all our prayers 17 must be based on obedience to God, regardless of our person, whether we be sinners or saints, worthy or unworthy. We must learn that 18 God will not have this commandment treated as a jest but will be angry and punish us if we do not pray, just as he punishes all other kinds of disobedience. Nor will he allow our prayers to be frustrated or lost, for if he did not intend to answer you, he would not have ordered you to pray and backed it up with such a strict commandment.

In the second place, we should be all the more urged and 19 encouraged to pray because God has promised that our prayer will surely be answered, as he says in Ps. 50:15, "Call upon me in the day of trouble, and I will deliver you," and Christ says in Matt. 7:7, 8, "Ask and it will be given you," etc. "For every one who asks receives." Such promises certainly ought to awaken and kindle in our hearts 20 a desire and love to pray. For by his Word God testifies that our prayer is heartily pleasing to him and will assuredly be heard and granted, so that we may not despise or disdain it or pray uncertainly.

This you can hold up to him and say, "I come to Thee, dear 21 Father, and pray not of my own accord or because of my own worthiness, but at thy commandment and promise, which cannot fail or deceive me." Whoever does not believe this promise should realize once again that he angers God, grossly dishonoring him and accusing him of falsehood.

Furthermore, we should be encouraged and drawn to pray 22 because, in addition to this commandment and promise, God takes the initiative and puts into our mouths the very words we are to use. Thus we see how sincerely he is concerned over our needs, and we

---

[8] Later edition adds: And I have just as great a need for it as those great saints—indeed, a greater need than they.

shall never doubt that our prayer pleases him and will assuredly be heard. So this prayer is far superior to all others that we might   23 ourselves devise. For in the latter our conscience would always be in doubt, saying, "I have prayed, but who knows whether it pleased him, or whether I have hit upon the right form and mode?" Thus there is no nobler prayer to be found on earth,[9] for it has the excellent testimony that God loves to hear it. This we should not trade for all the riches in the world.

It has been prescribed for this reason, also, that we should   24 reflect on our needs, which ought to drive and impel us to pray without ceasing. A person who wants to pray must present a petition, naming and asking for something which he desires; otherwise it cannot be called a prayer.

Therefore we have rightly rejected the prayers of monks and   25 priests, who howl and growl frightfully day and night; not one of them thinks of asking for the least thing. If we gathered all the churches together, with all their clergy, they would have to confess that they never prayed whole-heartedly for so much as a drop of wine. None of them has ever undertaken to pray out of obedience to God and faith in his promise, or out of consideration for his own needs. They only thought, at best, of doing a good work as a payment to God, not willing to receive anything from him, but only to give him something.

But where there is true prayer there must be earnestness. We   26 must feel our need, the distress that impels and drives us to cry out. Then prayer will come spontaneously, as it should, and we shall not need to be taught how to prepare for it or how to generate devotion. The need which ought to be the concern of both ourselves and   27 others is quite amply indicated in the Lord's Prayer. Therefore it may serve to remind us and impress upon us not to become negligent about praying. We all have needs enough, but the trouble is that we do not feel or see them. God therefore wishes you to lament and express your needs and wants, not because he is unaware of them, but in order that you may kindle your heart to stronger and greater desires and spread your cloak wide to receive many things.

Each of us should form the habit from his youth up to pray   28 daily for all his needs, whenever he is aware of anything that affects him or other people around him, such as preachers, magistrates, neighbors, servants; and, as we have said, he should always remind God of his commandment and promise, knowing that he will not have them despised. This I say because I would like to see the people   29 brought again to pray rightly and not act so crudely and coldly that they become daily more inept at praying. This is just what the devil

* Later edition adds: than the daily Lord's Prayer.

wants and works for with all his might, for he is well aware what damage and harm he suffers when prayer is in proper use.

This we must know, that all our safety and protection consist 30 in prayer alone. We are far too weak to cope with the devil and all his might and his forces arrayed against us, trying to trample us under foot. Therefore we must carefully select the weapons with which Christians ought to arm themselves in order to stand against the devil. What do you think has accomplished such great results in the 31 past, parrying the counsels and plots of our enemies and checking their murderous and seditious designs by which the devil expected to crush us, and the Gospel as well, except that the prayers of a few godly men intervened like an iron wall on our side? Otherwise they would have witnessed a far different drama: the devil would have destroyed all Germany in its own blood. Now they may confidently ridicule and mock. But by prayer alone we shall be a match both for them and for the devil, if we only persevere diligently and do not become slack. For whenever a good Christian prays, "Dear 32 Father, thy will be done," God replies from on high, "Yes, dear child, it shall indeed be done in spite of the devil and all the world."

Let this be said as an admonition in order that men may learn 33 above all to value prayer as a great and precious thing and may clearly distinguish between vain babbling and praying for something definite. We by no means reject prayer, but we do denounce the utterly useless howling and growling, as Christ himself rejects and forbids great wordiness.[1] Now we shall treat the Lord's Prayer very briefly and 34 clearly. In seven successive articles or petitions are comprehended all the needs that continually beset us, each one so great that it should impel us to keep praying for it all our lives.

[1] Matt. 6:7, 23:14.

THE INTRODUCTION

Our Father who art in heaven.

What does this mean?

Here God encourages us to believe
that he is truly our Father
and we are his children.

We therefore are to pray to him with
complete confidence
just as children speak to their loving
father.

THE FIRST PETITION

Hallowed be thy name.

What does this mean?

God's name certainly is holy in itself,
but we ask in this prayer
that we may keep it holy.

When does this happen?

God's name is hallowed
whenever his Word is taught
in its truth and purity
and we as children of God live in
harmony with it.
Help us to do this, heavenly Father!

But anyone who teaches or lives
contrary to the Word of God
dishonors God's name among us.
Keep us from doing this, heavenly
Father!

THE FIRST PETITION

"Hallowed be thy name."   35

This is rather obscure. It is not idiomatic German. In our   36
mother tongue we would say, "Heavenly Father, grant that thy name
alone may be holy." But what is it to pray that his name may   37
become holy? Is it not already holy? Answer: Yes, in itself it is
holy, but not in our use of it. God's name was given to us when we
became Christians at Baptism, and so we are called children of God
and enjoy the sacraments, through which he so incorporates us with
himself that all that is God's must serve for our use.

So we should realize that we are under the great necessity of   38
duly honoring his name and keeping it holy and sacred, regarding it
as the greatest treasure and most sacred thing we have, and praying,
as good children, that his name, which is already holy in heaven, may
also be kept holy on earth by us and all the world.

How does it become holy among us? The plainest answer is: 39
When both our teaching and our life are godly and Christian. Since in
this prayer we call God our Father, it is our duty in every way to
behave as good children so that he may receive from us not shame
but honor and praise.

Now, the name of God is profaned by us either in words or in   40
deeds; everything we do on earth may be classified as word or deed,
speech or act. In the first place, then, it is profaned when men   41
preach, teach, and speak in God's name anything that is false and
deceptive, using his name to cloak lies and make them acceptable; this
is the worst profanation and dishonor of the divine name. Like-   42
wise, when men grossly misuse the divine name as a cloak for their
shame, by swearing, cursing, conjuring, etc. In the next place, it is   43
also profaned by an openly evil life and wicked works, when those
who are called Christians and God's people are adulterers, drunkards,
gluttons, jealous persons, and slanderers. Here again God's name must
be profaned and blasphemed because of us.

Just as it is a shame and disgrace to an earthly father to have   44
a bad, unruly child who antagonizes him in word and deed with the
result that on his account the father suffers scorn and reproach, so God
is dishonored if we who are called by his name and enjoy his manifold
blessings fail to teach, speak, and live as godly and heavenly children
with the result that he must hear us called not children of God but
children of the devil.

So you see that in this petition we pray for exactly the same   45
thing that God demands in the Second Commandment: that his name
should not be taken in vain by swearing, cursing, deceiving, etc., but
used rightly to the praise and glory of God. Whoever uses God's name
for any sort of wrong profanes and desecrates this holy name, as in

the past a church was said to be desecrated when a murder or any other crime had been committed in it, or when a monstrance[2] or a relic was profaned, thus rendering unholy by misuse that which is holy in itself. This petition, then, is simple and clear as soon as we understand 46 the language, namely, that "to hallow" means the same as in our idiom "to praise, extol, and honor" in word and deed.

See, then, what a great need there is for this kind of prayer! 47 Since we see that the world is full of sects and false teachers, all of whom wear the holy name as a cloak and warrant for their devilish doctrine, we ought constantly to cry out against all who preach and believe falsely and against those who attack and persecute our Gospel and pure doctrine and try to suppress it, as the bishops, tyrants, fanatics, and others do. Likewise, this petition is for ourselves who have the Word of God but are ungrateful for it and fail to live according to it as we ought. If you pray the petition whole-heartedly, you can be 48 sure that God is pleased. For there is nothing he would rather hear than to have his glory and praise exalted above everything else and his Word taught in its purity and cherished and treasured.

---

[2] The monstrance was the vessel in which the host was displayed for adoration.

THE SECOND PETITION

Thy kingdom come.

What does this mean?

> God's kingdom comes indeed
> without our praying for it,
> but we ask in this prayer that it
>   may come also to us.

When does this happen?

> God's kingdom comes
> when our heavenly Father gives us his
>   Holy Spirit,
> so that by his grace we believe his
>   holy Word
> and live a godly life on earth now
>   and in heaven forever.

THE SECOND PETITION

"Thy kingdom come."

We prayed in the first petition that God would prevent the 49
world from using his glory and name to cloak its lies and wickedness,
but would rather keep God's name sacred and holy in both doctrine
and life so that he may be praised and exalted in us. Here we ask
that his kingdom may come. Just as God's name is holy in itself 50
and yet we pray that it may be holy among us, so also his kingdom
comes of itself without our prayer and yet we pray that it may come
to us. That is, we ask that it may prevail among us and with us, so
that we may be a part of those among whom his name is hallowed
and his kingdom flourishes.

What is the kingdom of God? Answer: Simply what we learned 51
in the Creed, namely, that God sent his Son, Christ our Lord, into the
world to redeem and deliver us from the power of the devil and to
bring us to himself and rule us as a king of righteousness, life, and

salvation against sin, death, and an evil conscience. To this end he also gave his Holy Spirit to teach us this through his holy Word and to enlighten and strengthen us in faith by his power.

We pray here at the outset that all this may be realized in us   52 and that God's name may be praised through his holy Word and our Christian lives. This we ask, both in order that we who have accepted it may remain faithful and grow daily in it and in order that it may gain recognition and followers among other people and advance with power throughout the world. So we pray that, led by the Holy Spirit, many may come into the kingdom of grace and become partakers of salvation, so that we may all remain together eternally in this kingdom which has now made its appearance among us.

God's kingdom comes to us in two ways: first, it comes here, in   53 time, through the Word and faith, and secondly, in eternity, it comes through the final revelation.[3] Now, we pray for both of these, that it may come to those who are not yet in it, and that it may come by daily growth here and in eternal life hereafter to us who have attained it. All this is simply to say: "Dear Father, we pray Thee, give us thy   54 Word, that the Gospel may be sincerely preached throughout the world and that it may be received by faith and may work and live in us. So we pray that thy kingdom may prevail among us through the Word and the power of the Holy Spirit, that the devil's kingdom may be overthrown and he may have no right or power over us, until finally the devil's kingdom shall be utterly destroyed and sin, death, and hell exterminated, and that we may live forever in perfect righteousness and blessedness."

You see that we are praying here not for a crust of bread or   55 for a temporal, perishable blessing, but for an eternal, priceless treasure and everything that God himself possesses. It would be far too great for any human heart to dare to desire if God himself had not commanded us to ask for it. But because he is God, he claims   56 the honor of giving far more abundantly and liberally than anyone can comprehend—like an eternal, inexhaustible fountain which, the more it gushes forth and overflows, the more it continues to give. He desires of us nothing more ardently than that we ask many and great things of him; and on the contrary, he is angered if we do not ask and demand confidently.

Imagine a very rich and mighty emperor who bade a poor   57 beggar to ask for whatever he might desire and was prepared to give great and princely gifts, and the fool asked only for a dish of beggar's broth. He would rightly be considered a rogue and a scoundrel who had made a mockery of his imperial majesty's command and was unworthy to come into his presence. Just so, it is a great reproach

---

[3] I.e., the return of Christ.

and dishonor to God if we, to whom he offers and pledges so many inexpressible blessings, despise them or lack confidence that we shall receive them and scarcely venture to ask for a morsel of bread.

The fault lies wholly in that shameful unbelief which does not 58 look to God even for enough to satisfy the belly, let alone expect, without doubting, eternal blesings from God. Therefore we must strengthen ourselves against unbelief and let the kingdom of God be the first thing for which we pray. Then, surely, we shall have all the other things in abundance, as Christ teaches, "Seek first the kingdom of God, and all these things shall be yours as well." [4] For how could God allow us to suffer want in temporal things when he promises that which is eternal and imperishable?

[4] Matt. 6:33.

THE THIRD PETITION

Thy will be done
on earth as it is in heaven.

What does this mean?

> The good and gracious will of God is
>   surely done without our prayer,
> but we ask in this prayer
> that it may be done also among us.

When does this happen?

> God's will is done when he hinders and
>   defeats every evil scheme and purpose
> of the devil, the world, and our sinful
>   self,
> which would prevent us from keeping
>   his name holy
> and would oppose the coming of his
>   kingdom.
> And his will is done
> when he strengthens our faith
> and keeps us firm in his Word as long as
>   we live.
> This is his gracious and good will.

THE THIRD PETITION

"Thy will be done on earth, as it is in heaven."   59

Thus far we have prayed that God's name may be hallowed by 60
us and that his kingdom may prevail among us. These two points
embrace all that pertains to God's glory and to our salvation, in which
we appropriate God with all his treasures. But there is just as great
need that we keep firm hold of these two things and never allow
ourselves to be torn from them. In a good government there is 61
need not only for good builders and rulers, but also for defenders,
protectors, and vigilant guardians. So here also; although we have

prayed for what is most essential—for the Gospel, for faith, and for the Holy Spirit, that he may govern us who have been redeemed from the power of the devil—we must also pray that God's will may be done. If we try to hold fast these treasures, we must suffer an astonishing amount of attacks and assaults from all who venture to hinder and thwart the fulfillment of the first two petitions.

It is unbelievable how the devil opposes and obstructs their 62 fulfillment. He cannot bear to have anyone teach or believe rightly. It pains him beyond measure when his lies and abominations, honored under the most specious pretexts of God's name, are disclosed and exposed in all their shame, when he himself is driven out of men's hearts and a breach is made in his kingdom. Therefore, like a furious foe, he raves and rages with all his power and might, marshaling all his subjects and even enlisting the world and our own flesh as his allies. For our flesh is in itself vile and inclined to evil, even when 63 we have accepted and believe God's Word. The world, too, is perverse and wicked. These he stirs up, fanning and feeding the flames, in order to hinder us, put us to flight, cut us down, and bring us once more under his power. This is his only purpose, his desire and 64 thought. For this end he strives without rest day and night, using all the arts, tricks, ways, and means that he can devise.

Therefore we who would be Christians must surely count on 65 having the devil with all his angels[5] and the world as our enemies and must count on their inflicting every possible misfortune and grief upon us. For where God's Word is preached, accepted or believed, and bears fruit, there the blessed holy cross will not be far away. Let nobody think that he will have peace; he must sacrifice all he has on earth—possessions, honor, house and home, wife and children, body and life. Now, this grieves our flesh and the old Adam, for it 66 means that we must remain steadfast, suffer patiently whatever befalls us, and let go whatever is taken from us.

Therefore, there is just as much need in this case as in every 67 other case to pray without ceasing: "Thy will be done, dear Father, and not the will of the devil or of our enemies, nor of those who would persecute and suppress thy holy Word or prevent thy kingdom from coming; and grant that whatever we must suffer on its account, we may patiently bear and overcome, so that our poor flesh may not yield or fall away through weakness or indolence."

Observe that in these three petitions interests which concern 68 God himself have been very simply expressed, yet we have prayed in our own behalf. What we pray for concerns only ourselves when we ask that what otherwise must be done without us may also be done in us. As God's name must be hallowed and his kingdom must come

[5] On the devil's angels, cf. Matt. 25:41.

even without our prayer, so must his will be done and prevail even though the devil and all his host storm and rage furiously against it in their attempt utterly to exterminate the Gospel. But for our own sake we must pray that his will may be done among us without hindrance, in spite of their fury, so that they may accomplish nothing and we may remain steadfast in the face of all violence and persecution, submitting to the will of God.

Such prayer must be our protection and defense now to repulse 69 and beat down all that the devil,[6] bishops, tyrants, and heretics can do against our Gospel. Let them all rage and do their worst, let them plot and plan how to suppress and exterminate us so that their will and scheme may prevail. One or two Christians, armed with this single petition, shall be our bulwark, against which the others shall dash themselves to pieces. It is our solace and boast that the will and 70 purpose of the devil and of all our enemies shall and must fail and come to naught, no matter how proud, secure, and powerful they think they are. For if their will were not broken and frustrated, the kingdom of God could not abide on earth nor his name be hallowed.

[6] Later version adds: pope.

THE FOURTH PETITION

Give us this day our daily bread.

What does this mean?

God gives daily bread, even without
    our prayer, to all people, though sinful,
but we ask in this prayer
that he will help us to realize this
and to receive our daily bread with
    thanks.

What is meant by "daily bread"?

Daily bread includes everything needed
    for this life,
such as food and clothing, home and
    property,
work and income, a devoted family,
an orderly community, good government,
favorable weather, peace and health,
a good name, and true friends and
    neighbors.

THE FOURTH PETITION

"Give us this day our daily bread."   71
Here we consider the poor bread-basket—the needs of our body 72
and our life on earth. It is a brief and simple word, but very
comprehensive. When you pray for "daily bread" you pray for everything that is necessary in order to have and enjoy daily bread and, on
the contrary, against everything that interferes with enjoying it. You
must therefore enlarge and extend your thoughts to include not only
the oven or the flour bin, but also the broad fields and the whole land
which produce and provide for us our daily bread and all kinds of
sustenance. For if God did not cause grain to grow and did not
bless and preserve it in the field, we could never take a loaf of bread
from the oven to set on the table.

To put it briefly, this petition includes everything that belongs   73
to our entire life in this world; only for its sake do we need daily bread.
Now, our life requires not only food and clothing and other necessities
for our body, but also peace and concord in our daily business and
in associations of every description with the people among whom we
live and move—in short, everything that pertains to the regulation of
our domestic and our civil or political affairs. For where these two
relations are interfered with and prevented from functioning properly,
there the necessities of life are also interfered with, and life itself cannot
be maintained for any length of time. Indeed, the greatest need of   74
all is to pray for our civil authorities and the government, for chiefly
through them does God provide us our daily bread and all the comforts
of this life. Although we have received from God all good things in
abundance, we cannot retain any of them or enjoy them in security
and happiness unless he gives us a stable, peaceful government. For
where dissension, strife, and war prevail, there our daily bread is taken
away, or at least reduced.

It would therefore be fitting if the coat-of-arms of every upright   75
prince were emblazoned with a loaf of bread instead of a lion or a
wreath of rue, or if a loaf of bread were stamped on coins, to remind
both princes and subjects that through the office of the princes we
enjoy protection and peace and that without them we could not have
the steady blessing of daily bread.[7] Rulers are worthy of all honor,
and we should render them the duties we owe and do all we can for
them, as to those through whom we enjoy our possessions in peace
and quietness, since otherwise we could not keep a penny. Moreover,
we should pray for them, that through them God may bestow on us
still more blessings and good things.

Let us outline very briefly how comprehensively this petition   76
covers all kinds of relations on earth. Out of it one might make a
long prayer, enumerating with many words all the things it includes.
For example, we might ask God to give us food and drink, clothing,
house, home, and a sound body; to cause the grain and fruits of the
field to grow and yield richly; to help us manage our household well
and give and preserve to us a good wife, children, and servants; to
cause our work, craft, or occupation, whatever it may be, to prosper
and succeed; to grant us faithful neighbors and good friends, etc.
Again, to ask God to endow the emperor, kings, and all estates of   77
men, and especially our princes, counselors, magistrates, and officials,
with wisdom, strength, and prosperity to govern well and to be
victorious over the Turks and all our enemies; to grant their subjects
and the people at large to live together in obedience, peace, and

---

[7] A black lion on gold appeared on the coat-of-arms of the March of
Meissen, a red and white striped lion on blue on that of the County of
Thuringia, a wreath of rue on that of Electoral Saxony. The *Löwenpfennig*
of Saxony and of Brunswick showed a lion on the coat-of-arms.

concord. On the other hand, to protect us from all kinds of harm   78
to our body and our livelihood, from tempest, hail, fire, and flood;
from poison, pestilence, and cattle-plague; from war and bloodshed,
famine, savage beasts, wicked men, etc. It is good to impress upon   79
the common people that all these things come from God and that we
must pray for them.

But especially is this petition directed against our chief enemy,   80
the devil, whose whole purpose and desire it is to take away or
interfere with all we have received from God. He is not satisfied to
obstruct and overthrow spiritual order, so that he may deceive men
with his lies and bring them under his power, but he also prevents
and hinders the establishment of any kind of government or honorable
and peaceful relations on earth. This is why he causes so much
contention, murder, sedition, and war, why he sends tempest and hail
to destroy crops and cattle, why he poisons the air, etc. In short,   81
it pains him that anyone receives a morsel of bread from God and
eats it in peace. If it were in his power, and our prayer to God did not
restrain him, surely we would not have a straw in the field, a penny
in the house, or even our life for one hour—especially those of us
who have the Word of God and would like to be Christians.

Thus, you see, God wishes to show us how he cares for us in   82
all our needs and faithfully provides for our daily existence.
Although he gives and provides these blessings bountifully, even   83
for wicked men and rogues, yet he wishes us to pray for them so we
may realize that we have received them from his hand and may
recognize in them his fatherly goodness toward us. When he withdraws
his hand, nothing can prosper or last for any length of time, as indeed
we see and experience every day. How much trouble there now   84
is in the world simply on account of false coinage, yes, on account of
daily exploitation and usury in public business, trading, and labor on
the part of those who wantonly oppress the poor and deprive them of
their daily bread! This we must put up with, of course; but let
exploiters and oppressors beware lest they lose the common intercession
of the church,[8] and let them take care lest this petition of the Lord's
Prayer be turned against them.

[8] The general prayer in the church. This was a kind of proverbial
expression, meaning "lose public respect."

THE FIFTH PETITION

And forgive us our trespasses,
as we forgive those who trespass
against us.

What does this mean?

> We ask in this prayer
> that our Father in heaven would not hold
>   our sins against us
> and because of them refuse to hear our
>   prayer.
>
> And we pray that he would give us
>   everything by grace,
> for we sin every day
> and deserve nothing but punishment.
>
> So we on our part will heartily forgive
> and gladly do good to those who sin
>   against us.

THE FIFTH PETITION

"And forgive us our debts, as we forgive our debtors."   85

This petition has to do with our poor, miserable life. Although   86
we have God's Word and believe, although we obey and submit to
his will and are supported by God's gift and blessing, nevertheless we
are not without sin. We still stumble daily and transgress because
we live in the world among people who sorely vex us and give us
occasion for impatience, wrath, vengeance, etc. Besides, Satan is   87
at our backs, besieging us on every side and, as we have heard,
directing his attacks against all the previous petitions, so that it is not
possible always to stand firm in such a ceaseless conflict.

Here again there is great need to call upon God and pray,   88
"Dear Father, forgive us our debts." Not that he does not forgive sin
even without and before our prayer; and he gave us the Gospel, in
which there is nothing but forgiveness, before we prayed or even

thought of it. But the point here is for us to recognize and accept this forgiveness. For the flesh in which we daily live is of such a 89 nature that it does not trust and believe God and is constantly aroused by evil desires and devices, so that we sin daily in word and deed, in acts of commission and omission. Thus our conscience becomes restless; it fears God's wrath and displeasure, and so it loses the comfort and confidence of the Gospel. Therefore it is necessary constantly to turn to this petition for the comfort that will restore our conscience.

This should serve God's purpose to break our pride and keep 90 us humble. He has reserved to himself this prerogative, that if anybody boasts of his goodness and despises others he should examine himself in the light of this petition. He will find that he is no better than others, that in the presence of God all men must humble themselves and be glad that they can attain forgiveness. Let no one think that he 91 will ever in this life reach the point where he does not need this forgiveness. In short, unless God constantly forgives, we are lost.

Thus this petition is really an appeal to God not to regard our 92 sins and punish us as we daily deserve, but to deal graciously with us, forgive as he has promised, and thus grant us a happy and cheerful conscience to stand before him in prayer. Where the heart is not right with God and cannot achieve such confidence, it will never dare to pray. But such a confident and joyful heart can only come from the knowledge that our sins are forgiven.

Meanwhile, a necessary but comforting clause is added, "as we 93 forgive our debtors." God has promised us assurance that everything is forgiven and pardoned, yet on the condition that we also forgive our neighbor. Inasmuch as we sin greatly against God everyday 94 and yet he forgives it all through grace, we must always forgive our neighbor who does us harm, violence, and injustice, bears malice toward us, etc. If you do not forgive, do not think that God 95 forgives you. But if you forgive, you have the comfort and assurance that you are forgiven in heaven. Not on account of your forgiving, 96 for God does it altogether freely, out of pure grace, because he has promised it, as the Gospel teaches. But he has set up this condition for our strengthening and assurance as a sign along with the promise which is in agreement with this petition, Luke 6:37, "Forgive, and you will be forgiven." Therefore Christ repeats it immediately after the Lord's Prayer in Matt. 6:14, saying, "If you forgive men their trespasses, your heavenly Father also will forgive you," etc.

This sign is attached to the petition, therefore, that when we 97 pray we may recall the promise and think, "Dear Father, I come to Thee praying for forgiveness, not because I can make satisfaction or merit anything by my works, but because Thou hast given the promise and hast set thy seal to it, making it as certain as an absolution

pronounced by thyself." Whatever can be effected by Baptism   98
and the Lord's Supper, which are appointed as outward signs, this
sign also can effect to strengthen and gladden our conscience. And
it has been especially instituted for us to use and practice every hour,
keeping it with us at all times.

THE SIXTH PETITION

And lead us not into temptation.

What does this mean?

> God tempts no one to sin,
> but we ask in this prayer that God would
>   watch over us and keep us
> so that the devil, the world, and our
>   sinful self may not deceive us
> and draw us into false belief, despair,
>   and other great and shameful sins.

> And we pray that even though we are
>   so tempted
> we may still win the final victory.

THE SIXTH PETITION

"And lead us not into temptation."   99

We have now heard enough about the trouble and effort 100 required to retain and persevere in all the gifts for which we pray. This, however, is not accomplished without failures and stumbling. Moreover, although we have acquired forgiveness and a good conscience, and have been wholly absolved, yet such is life that one stands today and falls tomorrow. Therefore, even though at present we are upright and stand before God with a good conscience, we must pray again that he will not allow us to fall and yield to trials and temptations.

Temptation (or, as the ancient Saxons called it, *Bekörunge*)[9] 101 is of three kinds: of the flesh, the world, and the devil. We live 102 in the flesh and we have the old Adam hanging around our necks; he goes to work and lures us daily into unchastity, laziness, gluttony and drunkenness, greed and deceit, into acts of fraud and deception against our neighbor—in short, into all kinds of evil lusts which by nature cling to us and to which we are incited by the association and example

[9] By Saxony Luther meant Lower Saxony; in the sixteenth century *Plattdeutsch* was spoken in Wittenberg. In the Latin Book of Concord *Bekörunge* was misunderstood as *Bekehrung, conversio.*

of other people and by things we hear and see. All this often wounds and inflames even an innocent heart.

Next comes the world, which assails us by word and deed and |03 drives us to anger and impatience. In short, there is in it nothing but hatred and envy, enmity, violence and injustice, perfidy, vengeance, cursing, reviling, slander, arrogance, and pride, along with fondness for luxury, honor, fame, and power. No one is willing to be the least, but everyone wants to sit in the chief seat and be seen by all.

Then comes the devil, who baits and badgers us on all sides, |04 but especially exerts himself where the conscience and spiritual matters are at stake. His purpose is to make us scorn and despise both the Word and the works of God, to tear us away from faith, hope, and love, to draw us into unbelief, false security, and stubbornness, or, on the contrary, to drive us into despair, atheism, blasphemy, and countless other abominable sins. These are snares and nets; indeed, they are the real "flaming darts" [1] which are venomously shot into our hearts, not by flesh and blood but by the devil.

These are the great, grievous perils and temptations which |05 every Christian must bear, even if they come one by one. As long as we remain in this vile life in which we are attacked, hunted, and harried on all sides, we are constrained to cry out and pray every hour that God may not allow us to become faint and weary and to fall back into sin, shame, and unbelief. Otherwise it is impossible to overcome even the least temptation.

This, then, is "leading us not into temptation" when God |06 gives us power and strength to resist, even though the tribulation is not removed or ended. For no one can escape temptations and allurements as long as we live in the flesh and have the devil prowling about us. We cannot help but suffer tribulations, and even be entangled in them, but we pray here that we may not fall into them and be overwhelmed by them.

To feel temptation, therefore, is quite a different thing from |07 consenting and yielding to it. We must all feel it, though not all to the same degree; some have more frequent and severe temptations than others. Youths, for example, are tempted chiefly by the flesh; older people are tempted by the world. Others, who are concerned with spiritual matters (that is, strong Christians) are tempted by the devil. But we cannot be harmed by the mere feeling of temptation as |08 long as it is contrary to our will and and we would prefer to be rid of it. If we did not feel it, it could not be called a temptation. But to consent to it is to give it free rein and neither resist it nor pray for help against it.

Accordingly we Christians must be armed and prepared for |09

[1] Cf. Eph. 6:16.

incessant attacks. Then we shall not go about securely and heedlessly as if the devil were far from us but shall at all times expect his blows and parry them. Even if at present I am chaste, patient, kind, and firm in faith, the devil is likely in this very hour to send such a shaft into my heart that I can scarcely stand, for he is an enemy who never stops or becomes weary; when one attack ceases, new ones always arise.

At such times your only help or comfort is to take refuge in 110 the Lord's Prayer and to appeal to God from your heart, "Dear Father, Thou hast commanded me to pray; let me not fall because of temptation." Then you will see the temptation cease and eventually 111 admit defeat. Otherwise, if you attempt to help yourself by your own thoughts and counsels, you will only make the matter worse and give the devil a better opening. For he has a serpent's head; if it finds an opening into which it can slip, the whole body will irresistibly follow. But prayer can resist him and drive him back.

THE SEVENTH PETITION

But deliver us from evil.

What does this mean?

> We ask in this inclusive prayer
> that our heavenly Father would save us
>   from every evil to body and soul,
> and at our last hour would mercifully
>   take us
> from the troubles of this world to himself
>   in heaven.

THE DOXOLOGY

For thine is the kingdom
and the power and the glory
forever and ever. Amen.

What does "Amen" mean?

> *Amen* means *Yes, it shall be so.*
> We say *Amen* because we are certain
> that such petitions are pleasing to our
>   Father in heaven and are heard by him.
> For he himself has commanded us to
>   pray in this way
> and has promised to hear us.

THE LAST PETITION

"But deliver us from evil. Amen."   112

In the Greek[2] this petition reads, "Deliver or keep us from   113
the Evil One, or the Wicked One." The petition seems to be speaking
of the devil as the sum of all evil in order that the entire substance
of our prayer may be directed against our arch-enemy. It is he who
obstructs everything that we pray for: God's name or glory, God's
kingdom and will, our daily bread, a good and cheerful conscience, etc.

Therefore we sum it all up by saying, "Dear Father, help us to   114

---

[2] The first edition of the Large Catechism reads erroneously, "In the
Hebrew."

get rid of all this misfortune." Nevertheless, this petition includes |15
all the evil that may befall us under the devil's kingdom: poverty,
shame, death, and, in short, all the tragic misery and heartache of
which there is so incalculably much on earth. Since the devil is not
only a liar but also a murderer,[3] he incessantly seeks our life and
vents his anger by causing accidents and injury to our bodies. He
breaks many a man's neck and drives others to insanity; some he
drowns, and many he hounds to suicide or other dreadful catastrophes.
Therefore there is nothing for us to do on earth but to pray |16
constantly against this arch-enemy. For if God did not support us, we
would not be safe from him for a single hour.

Thus you see how God wants us to pray to him for every- |17
thing that affects our bodily welfare and directs us to seek and expect
help from no one but him. But this petition he has put last, for |18
if we are to be protected and delivered from all evil, his name must
first be hallowed in us, his kingdom come among us, and his will be
done. Then he will preserve us from sin and shame and from everything else that harms or injures us.

Thus God has briefly set before us all the afflictions that may |19
ever beset us in order that we may never have an excuse for failing
to pray. But the efficacy of prayer consists in our learning also to say
"Amen" to it—that is, not to doubt that our prayer is surely heard and
will be granted. This word is nothing else than an unquestioning |20
affirmation of faith on the part of one who does not pray as a matter of
chance but knows that God does not lie since he has promised to grant
his requests. Where such faith is wanting, there can be no true prayer.

It is therefore a pernicious delusion when people pray in such |21
a way that they dare not whole-heartedly add "yes" and conclude with
certainty that God hears their prayer but remain in doubt, saying,
"Why should I be so bold as to boast that God hears my prayer? I am
only a poor sinner," etc. That means that they have their eye |22
not on God's promise but on their own works and worthiness, so that
they despise God and accuse him of lying. Therefore they receive |23
nothing, as St. James says, "If anyone prays, let him ask in faith, with
no doubting, for he who doubts is like a wave of the sea that is driven
and tossed by the wind. For that person must not suppose that he
will receive anything from God." [4] Behold, such is the impor- |24
tance that God attaches to our being certain that we do not pray in
vain and that we must not in any way despise our prayers.

[3] John 8:44.
[4] James 1:6, 7.

1

What is Baptism?

Baptism is not water only,
but it is water used together with God's
Word and by his command.

What is this Word?

In Matthew 28 our Lord Jesus Christ says:

"Go therefore and make disciples of all
nations,
baptizing them in the name of the Father
and of the Son and of the Holy Spirit."

2

What benefits does God give in Baptism?

In Baptism God forgives sin,
delivers from death and the devil,
and gives everlasting salvation to all who
believe what he has promised.

What is God's promise?

In Mark 16 our Lord Jesus Christ says:

"He who believes and is baptized will be
saved;
but he who does not believe will be
condemned."

3

How can water do such great things?

It is not water that does these things,
but God's Word with the water and our
trust in this Word.
Water by itself is only water,
but with the Word of God

it is a life-giving water
which by grace gives the new birth
   through the Holy Spirit.

St. Paul writes in Titus 3:

"He saved us . . . in virtue of his own mercy,
by the washing of regeneration and renewal
   in the Holy Spirit,
which he poured out upon us richly
through Jesus Christ our Savior,
so that we might be justified by his grace
and become heirs in hope of eternal life.
The saying is sure."

4

What does Baptism mean for daily living?

It means that our sinful self, with all its
   evil deeds and desires,
should be drowned through daily
   repentance;
and that day after day a new self should
   arise
to live with God in righteousness and
   purity forever.

St. Paul writes in Romans 6:

"We were buried therefore with him by
   Baptism into death,
so that as Christ was raised from the dead
   by the glory of the Father,
we too might walk in newness of life."

We have now finished with the three chief parts[5] of our common |
Christian teaching. It remains for us to speak of our two sacraments,
instituted by Christ. Every Christian ought to have at least some brief,
elementary instruction in them because without these no one can be
a Christian, although unfortunately in the past nothing was taught
about them. First we shall take up Baptism, through which we   2
are first received into the Christian community. In order that it may
be readily understood, we shall treat it in a systematic way and confine
ourselves to that which is necessary for us to know. How it is to be
maintained and defended against heretics and sectarians we shall
leave to the learned.

In the first place, we must above all be familiar with the words   3
upon which Baptism is founded and to which everything is related
that is to be said on the subject, namely, where the Lord Christ says
in Matt. 28:19,

"Go into all the world, and teach all nations, baptizing them in   4
the name of the Father and of the Son and of the Holy Spirit."

Likewise in Mark 16:16,

"He who believes and is baptized will be saved; but he who   5
does not believe will be condemned."

Observe, first, that these words contain God's commandment   6
and ordinance. You should not doubt, then, that Baptism is of divine
origin, not something devised or invented by men. As truly as I can
say that the Ten Commandments, the Creed, and the Lord's Prayer
are not spun out of any man's imagination but revealed and given
by God himself, so I can also boast that Baptism is no human play-
thing but is instituted by God himself. Moreover, it is solemnly and
strictly commanded that we must be baptized or we shall not be saved.
We are not to regard it as an indifferent matter, then, like putting on
a new red coat. It is of the greatest importance that we regard   7
Baptism as excellent, glorious, and exalted. It is the chief cause of
our contentions and battles because the world now is full of sects who
proclaim that Baptism is an external thing and that external things are
of no use.[6] But no matter how external it may be, here stand   8
God's Word and command which have instituted, established, and
confirmed Baptism. What God institutes and commands cannot be
useless. It is a most precious thing, even though to all appearances it
may not be worth a straw. If people used to consider it a great   9
thing when the pope dispensed indulgences with his letters and bulls
and consecrated altars and churches solely by virtue of his letters and
seals, then we ought to regard Baptism as much greater and more

---

[5] Luther used the word *Hauptstücke* in a double sense: "major divisions"
but also "chief articles" or "the most essential." Cf. above, Large Catechism,
II, 6, and Small Catechism, VI, 8.

[6] This was an argument used by some left-wing radicals in the sixteenth
century.

precious because God has commanded it and, what is more, it is performed in his name. So the words read, "Go, baptize," not in your name but "in God's name."

To be baptized in God's name is to be baptized not by men   10 but by God himself. Although it is performed by men's hands, it is nevertheless truly God's own act. From this fact everyone can easily conclude that it is of much greater value than the work of any man or saint. For what work can man do that is greater than God's work?

Here the devil sets to work to blind us with false appearances   11 and lead us away from God's work to our own. It makes a much more splendid appearance when a Carthusian[7] does many great and difficult works, and we all attach greater importance to our own achievements and merits. But the Scriptures teach that if we piled   12 together all the works of all the monks, no matter how precious and dazzling they might appear, they would not be as noble and good as if God were to pick up a straw. Why? Because the person performing the act is nobler and better. Here we must evaluate not the person according to the works, but the works according to the person, from whom they must derive their worth. But mad reason rushes forth[8]   13 and, because Baptism is not dazzling like the works which we do, regards it as worthless.

Now you can understand how to answer properly the question,   14 What is Baptism? It is not simply common water, but water comprehended in God's Word and commandment and sanctified by them. It is nothing else than a divine water, not that the water in itself is nobler than other water but that God's Word and commandment are added to it.

Therefore it is sheer wickedness and devilish blasphemy when   15 our new spirits, in order to slander Baptism, ignore God's Word and ordinance, consider nothing but the water drawn from the well, and then babble, "How can a handful of water help the soul?" Of   16 course, my friend! Who does not know that water is water, if such a separation is proper? But how dare you tamper thus with God's ordinance and tear from it the precious jeweled clasp with which God has fastened and enclosed it and from which he does not wish his ordinance to be separated? For the nucleus in the water is God's Word or commandment and God's name, and this is a treasure greater and nobler than heaven and earth.

Note the distinction, then: Baptism is a very different thing   17 from all other water, not by virtue of the natural substance but because here something nobler is added. God himself stakes his honor, his power, and his might on it. Therefore it is not simply a natural water,

[7] See above, Ten Commandments, 74 and footnote.
[8] Later version: But mad reason will not listen to this.

but a divine, heavenly, holy, and blessed water—praise it in any other terms you can—all by virtue of the Word, which is a heavenly, holy Word which no one can sufficiently extol, for it contains and conveys all the fullness of God. From the Word it derives its nature as a 18 sacrament, as St. Augustine taught, *"Accedat verbum ad elementum et fit sacramentum."* [9] This means that when the Word is added to the element or the natural substance, it becomes a sacrament, that is, a holy, divine thing and sign.

Therefore, we constantly teach that the sacraments and all the 19 external things ordained and instituted by God should be regarded not according to the gross, external mask (as we see the shell of a nut) but as that in which God's Word is enclosed. In the same way 20 we speak about the parental estate and civil authority. If we regard these persons with reference to their noses, eyes, skin and hair, flesh and bones, they look no different from Turks and heathen. Someone might come and say, "Why should I think more of this person than of others?" But because the commandment is added, "You shall honor father and mother," I see another man, adorned and clothed with the majesty and glory of God. The commandment, I say, is the golden chain about his neck, yes, the crown on his head, which shows me how and why I should honor this particular flesh and blood.

In the same manner, and even much more, you should honor 21 and exalt Baptism on account of the Word, since God himself has honored it by words and deeds and has confirmed it by wonders from heaven. Do you think it was a jest that the heavens opened when Christ allowed himself to be baptized, that the Holy Spirit descended visibly,[1] and that the divine glory and majesty were manifested everywhere?

I therefore admonish you again that these two, the Word and 22 the water, must by no means be separated from each other. For where the Word is separated from the water, the water is no different from that which the maid cooks with and could indeed be called a bath-keeper's baptism.[2] But when the Word is present according to God's ordinance, Baptism is a sacrament, and it is called Christ's Baptism. This is the first point to be emphasized: the nature and dignity of this holy sacrament.

In the second place, since we now know what Baptism is and 23 how it is to be regarded, we must also learn for what purpose it was instituted, that is, what benefits, gifts, and effects it brings. Nor can we understand this better than from the words of Christ quoted above,

---

[9] *Tractate 80,* on John 3.
[1] Matt. 3:16.
[2] Cf. Luther's "Sermon on Baptism" (1534): "a mere watery or earthly water, or (as the sectarians call it) a bath-water or dog's bath." *WA,* 37:642.

"He who believes and is baptized shall be saved." [3] To put it 24
most simply, the power, effect, benefit, fruit, and purpose of Baptism
is to save. No one is baptized in order to become a prince, but as
the words say, to "be saved." To be saved, we know, is nothing 25
else than to be delivered from sin, death, and the devil and to enter
into the kingdom of Christ and live with him forever.

Here you see again how precious and important a thing Baptism 26
should be regarded as being, for in it we obtain such an inexpressible
treasure. This shows that it is not simple, ordinary water, for ordinary
water could not have such an effect. But the Word has. It shows also
(as we said above) that God's name is in it. And where God's 27
name is, there must also be life and salvation. Hence it is well described as a divine, blessed, fruitful, and gracious water, for through
the Word Baptism receives the power to become the "washing of
regeneration," as St. Paul calls it in Titus 3:5.

Our know-it-alls, the new spirits,[4] assert that faith alone saves 28
and that works and external things contribute nothing to this end.
We answer: It is true, nothing that is in us does it but faith, as we
shall hear later on. But these leaders of the blind are unwilling 29
to see that faith must have something to believe—something to which
it may cling and upon which it may stand. Thus faith clings to the
water and believes it to be Baptism in which there is sheer salvation
and life, not through the water, as we have sufficiently stated, but
through its incorporation with God's Word and ordinance and the
joining of his name to it. When I believe this, what else is it but
believing in God as the one who has implanted his Word in this external ordinance and offered it to us so that we may grasp the treasure
it contains?

Now, these people are so foolish as to separate faith from 30
the object to which faith is attached and bound on the ground that the
object is something external. Yes, it must be external so that it can
be perceived and grasped by the senses and thus brought into the
heart, just as the entire Gospel is an external, oral proclamation. In
short, whatever God effects in us he does through such external ordinances. No matter where he speaks—indeed, no matter for what purpose or by what means he speaks—there faith must look and to it
faith must hold. We have here the words, "He who believes and 31
is baptized will be saved." To what do they refer but to Baptism, that
is, the water comprehended in God's ordinance? Hence it follows that
whoever rejects Baptism rejects God's Word, faith, and Christ, who
directs us and binds us to Baptism.

In the third place, having learned the great benefit and power 32
of Baptism, let us observe further who receives these gifts and benefits

[3] Mark 16:16.
[4] Zwinglians or Anabaptists.

of Baptism. This again is most beautifully and clearly expressed   33
in these same words, "He who believes and is baptized will be saved,"
that is, faith alone makes the person worthy to receive the salutary,
divine water profitably. Since these blessings are offered and promised
in the words which accompany the water, they cannot be received
unless we believe them whole-heartedly. Without faith Baptism   34
is of no use, although in itself it is an infinite, divine treasure. So this
single expression, "He who believes," is so potent that it excludes and
rejects all works that we may do with the intention of meriting salvation through them. For it is certain that whatever is not faith con-
tributes nothing toward salvation, and receives nothing.

However, it is often objected, "If Baptism is itself a work, and   35
you say that works are of no use for salvation, what becomes of
faith?" To this you may answer: Yes, it is true that our works are
of no use for salvation. Baptism, however, is not our work but God's
(for, as was said, you must distinguish Christ's Baptism quite clearly
from a bath-keeper's baptism). God's works, however, are salutary
and necessary for salvation, and they do not exclude but rather demand[5] faith, for without faith they could not be grasped. Just by   36
allowing the water to be poured over you, you do not receive Baptism
in such a manner that it does you any good. But it becomes beneficial
to you if you accept it as God's command and ordinance, so that,
baptized in the name of God, you may receive in the water the
promised salvation. This the hand cannot do, nor the body, but the
heart must believe it.

Thus you see plainly that Baptism is not a work which we do   37
but is a treasure which God gives us and faith grasps, just as the Lord
Christ upon the cross is not a work but a treasure comprehended and
offered to us in the Word and received by faith. Therefore they are
unfair when they cry out against us as though we preach against faith.
Actually, we insist on faith alone as so necessary that without it nothing
can be received or enjoyed.

Thus we have considered the three things that must be known   38
about this sacrament, especially that it is God's ordinance and is to
be held in all honor. This alone would be enough, even though
Baptism is an entirely external thing. Similarly the commandment,
"You shall honor your father and mother," refers only to human
flesh and blood, yet we look not at the flesh and blood but at God's
commandment in which it is comprehended and on account of which
this flesh is called father and mother. Just so, if we had nothing more
than these words, "Go and baptize," we would still have to accept and
observe Baptism as an ordinance of God. But here we have not   39
only God's commandment and injunction, but also his promise. There-

---

[5] Luther's word *fodern* may mean both "demand" (*forden*) and "further"
(*fördern*). Obsopoeus' Latin translation of the Catechism understood the
word here as "demand."

fore, it is far more glorious than anything else God has commanded
and ordained; in short, it is so full of comfort and grace that heaven
and earth cannot comprehend it. It takes special understanding   40
to believe this, for it is not the treasure that is lacking; rather, what is
lacking is that it should be grasped and held firmly.

In Baptism, therefore, every Christian has enough to study and   41
to practice all his life. He always has enough to do to believe firmly
what Baptism promises and brings—victory over death and the devil,
forgiveness of sin, God's grace, the entire Christ, and the Holy Spirit
with his gifts. In short, the blessings of Baptism are so boundless   42
that if timid nature considers them, it may well doubt whether they
could all be true. Suppose there were a physician who had such   43
skill that people would not die, or even though they died[6] would afterward live forever. Just think how the world would snow and rain
money upon him! Because of the pressing crowd of rich men no one
else could get near him. Now, here in Baptism there is brought free
to every man's door just such a priceless medicine which swallows up
death[7] and saves the lives of all men.

To appreciate and use Baptism aright, we must draw strength   44
and comfort from it when our sins or conscience oppress us, and we
must retort, "But I am baptized! And if I am baptized, I have the
promise that I shall be saved and have eternal life, both in soul and
body." This is the reason why these two things are done in   45
Baptism: the body has water poured over it, though it cannot receive
anything but the water, and meanwhile the Word is spoken so that
the soul may grasp it.

Since the water and the Word together constitute one Baptism,   46
body and soul shall be saved and live forever: the soul through the
Word in which it believes, the body because it is united with the soul
and apprehends Baptism in the only way it can. No greater jewel,
therefore, can adorn our body and soul than Baptism, for through it
we obtain perfect holiness and salvation, which no other kind of life
and no work on earth can acquire.

Let this suffice concerning the nature, benefits, and use of Baptism
as answering the present purpose.

[INFANT BAPTISM] [8]

Here we come to a question by which the devil confuses the   47
world through his sects, the question of infant Baptism. Do children
also believe, and is it right to baptize them? To this we reply   48
briefly: Let the simple dismiss this question from their minds and
refer it to the learned. But if you wish to answer, then say:

[6] Later version adds: would be restored to life and.
[7] Isa. 25·8.
[8] Title added in the German Book of Concord.

That the Baptism of infants is pleasing to Christ is sufficiently   49
proved from his own work. God has sanctified many who have been
thus baptized and has given them the Holy Spirit. Even today there
are not a few whose doctrine and life attest that they have the Holy
Spirit. Similarly by God's grace we have been given the power to
interpret the Scriptures and to know Christ, which is impossible without the Holy Spirit. Now, if God did not accept the Baptism of   50
infants, he would not have given any of them the Holy Spirit nor any
part of him; in short, all this time down to the present day no man
on earth could have been a Christian. Since God has confirmed Baptism through the gift of his Holy Spirit, as we have perceived in some
of the fathers, such as St. Bernard, Gerson, John Hus, and others,[9]
and since the holy Christian church will abide until the end of the
world, our adversaries must acknowledge that infant Baptism is pleasing to God. For he can never be in conflict with himself, support
lies and wickedness, or give his grace and Spirit for such ends. This   51
is the best and strongest proof for the simple and unlearned. For no
one can take from us or overthrow this article, "I believe one holy
Christian church, the communion of saints," etc.

Further, we are not primarily concerned whether the baptized   52
person believes or not, for in the latter case Baptism does not become
invalid. Everything depends upon the Word and commandment   53
of God. This, perhaps, is a rather subtle point, but it is based upon
what I have already said, that Baptism is simply water and God's
Word in and with each other; that is, when the Word accompanies
the water, Baptism is valid, even though faith be lacking. For my
faith does not constitute Baptism but receives it. Baptism does not
become invalid even if it is wrongly received or used, for it is bound
not to our faith but to the Word.

Even though a Jew should today come deceitfully and with   54
an evil purpose, and we baptized him in all good faith, we should
have to admit that his Baptism was valid. For there would be water
together with God's Word, even though he failed to receive it properly.
Similarly, those who partake unworthily of the Lord's Supper receive
the true sacrament even though they do not believe.

So you see that the objection of the sectarians is absurd. As   55
we said, even if infants did not believe—which, however, is not the
case, as we have proved—still their Baptism would be valid and no
one should rebaptize them. Similarly, the Sacrament of the Altar is
not vitiated if someone approaches it with an evil purpose, and he
would not be permitted on account of that abuse to take it again the
selfsame hour, as if he had not really received the sacrament the first
time. That would be to blaspheme and desecrate the sacrament in the

[9] Later version adds: who were baptized in infancy.

worst way. How dare we think that God's Word and ordinance should be wrong and invalid because we use it wrongly?

Therefore, I say, if you did not believe before, then believe 56 afterward and confess, "The Baptism indeed was right, but unfortunately I did not receive it rightly." I myself, and all who are baptized, must say before God: "I come here in my faith, and in the faith of others, nevertheless I cannot build on the fact that I believe and many people are praying for me. On this I build, that it is thy Word and command." Just so, I go to the Sacrament of the Altar not on the strength of my own faith, but on the strength of Christ's Word. I may be strong or weak; I leave that in God's hands. This I know, however, that he has commanded me to go, eat, and drink, etc. and that he gives me his body and blood; he will not lie or deceive me.

We do the same in infant Baptism. We bring the child with 57 the purpose and hope that he may believe, and we pray God to grant him faith. But we do not baptize him on that account, but solely on the command of God. Why? Because we know that God does not lie. My neighbor and I—in short, all men—may err and deceive, but God's Word cannot err.

Therefore only presumptuous and stupid persons draw the 58 conclusion that where there is no true faith, there also can be no true Baptism. Likewise I might argue, "If I have no faith, then Christ is nothing." Or again, "If I am not obedient, then father, mother, and magistrates are nothing." Is it correct to conclude that when anybody does not do what he should, the thing that he misuses has no existence or no value? My friend, rather invert the argument and conclude, 59 Precisely because Baptism has been wrongly received, it has existence and value. The saying goes, *"Abusus non tollit, sed confirmat substantiam,"* that is, "Misuse does not destroy the substance, but confirms its existence." Gold remains no less gold if a harlot wears it in sin and shame.

Let the conclusion therefore be that Baptism always remains 60 valid and retains its integrity, even if only one person were baptized and he, moreover, did not have true faith. For God's ordinance and Word cannot be changed or altered by man. But these fanatics 61 are so blinded that they do not discern God's Word and commandment. They regard Baptism only as water in the brook or in the pot, and magistrates only as ordinary people. And because they see neither faith nor obedience, they conclude that these ordinances are in themselves invalid. Here lurks a sneaky, seditious devil who would 62 like to snatch the crown from the rulers and trample it under foot and would, in addition, pervert and nullify all God's work and ordinances. We must therefore be watchful and well armed and not 63 allow ourselves to be turned aside from the Word, regarding Baptism merely as an empty sign, as the fanatics dream.

Finally, we must know what Baptism signifies and why God   64
ordained just this sign and external observance for the sacrament by
which we are first received into the Christian church. This act or   65
observance consists in being dipped into the water, which covers us
completely, and being drawn out again. These two parts, being dipped
under the water and emerging from it, indicate the power and effect
of Baptism, which is simply the slaying of the old Adam and the
resurrection of the new man, both of which actions must continue in
us our whole life long. Thus a Christian life is nothing else than a
daily Baptism, once begun and ever continued. For we must keep
at it incessantly, always purging out whatever pertains to the old
Adam, so that whatever belongs to the new man may come forth.
What is the old man? He is what is born in us from Adam,   66
irascible, spiteful, envious, unchaste, greedy, lazy, proud, yes, and
unbelieving; he is beset with all vices and by nature has nothing good
in him. Now, when we enter Christ's kingdom, this corruption   67
must daily decrease so that the longer we live the more gentle, patient,
and meek we become, and the more free from greed, hatred, envy,
and pride.

This is the right use of Baptism among Christians, signified by   68
baptizing with water. Where this amendment of life does not take
place but the old man is given free rein and continually grows stronger,
Baptism is not being used but resisted. Those who are outside of   69
Christ can only grow worse day by day. It is as the proverb says
very truly, "Evil unchecked becomes worse and worse." If a year   70
ago a man was proud and greedy, this year he is much more so. Vice
thus grows and increases in him from his youth up. A young child,
who has no particular vice, becomes vicious and unchaste as he grows.
When he reaches full manhood, the real vices become more and more
potent day by day.

The old man therefore follows unchecked the inclinations of   71
his nature if he is not restrained and suppressed by the power of
Baptism. On the other hand, when we become Christians, the old man
daily decreases until he is finally destroyed. This is what it means to
plunge into Baptism and daily come forth again. So the external   72
sign has been appointed not only on account of what it confers, but
also on account of what it signifies. Where faith is present with its   73
fruits, there Baptism is no empty symbol, but the effect accompanies
it; but where faith is lacking, it remains a mere unfruitful sign.

Here you see that Baptism, both by its power and by its   74
signification, comprehends also the third sacrament, formerly called
Penance,[1] which is really nothing else than Baptism. What is   75

---

[1] *Penitentia* (*Busse*) in the Roman Catholic system meant both the

repentance but an earnest attack on the old man and an entering upon a new life? If you live in repentance, therefore, you are walking in Baptism, which not only announces this new life but also produces, begins, and promotes it. In Baptism we are given the grace, Spirit, 76 and power to suppress the old man so that the new may come forth and grow strong.

Therefore Baptism remains forever. Even though we fall from 77 it and sin, nevertheless we always have access to it so that we may again subdue the old man. But we need not again have the water 78 poured over us. Even if we were immersed in water a hundred times, it would nevertheless be only one Baptism, and the effect and signification of Baptism would continue and remain. Repentance, therefore, is 79 nothing else than a return and approach to Baptism, to resume and practice what had earlier been begun but abandoned.

I say this to correct the opinion, which has long prevailed 80 among us, that our Baptism is something past which we can no longer use after falling again into sin. We have such a notion because we regard Baptism only in the light of a work performed once for all. Indeed, St. Jerome is responsible for this view, for he wrote, 81 "Repentance is the second plank[2] on which we must swim ashore after the ship founders" in which we embarked when we entered the Christian church.[3] This interpretation deprives Baptism of its 82 value, making it of no further use to us. Therefore the statement is incorrect.[4] The ship does not founder since, as we said, it is God's ordinance and not a work of ours. But it does happen that we slip and fall out of the ship. If anybody does fall out, he should immediately head for the ship and cling to it until he can climb aboard again and sail on in it as he had done before.

Thus we see what a great and excellent thing Baptism is, which 83 snatches us from the jaws of the devil and makes God our own, overcomes and takes away sin and daily strengthens the new man, always remains until we pass from this present misery to eternal glory.

Therefore let everybody regard his Baptism as the daily 84 garment which he is to wear all the time. Every day he should be found in faith and amid its fruits, every day he should be suppressing the old man and growing up in the new. If we wish to be 85 Christians, we must practice the work that makes us Christians. But if anybody falls away from his Baptism let him return to it. 86

sacrament (Penance) and the act of satisfaction enjoined by the priest (penance) and the inward attitude of repentance.

[2] Baptism was regarded as the first plank.

[3] Epistle 130 to Demetrias. Cf. also Epistle 122 to Rusticus, **Epistle 147 to** Fallen Sabinianus, and Commentary on Isaiah, ch. 3, 8-9.

[4] Later version adds: or else was never rightly understood.

As Christ, the mercy-seat,[5] does not recede from us or forbid us to return to him even though we sin, so all his treasures and gifts remain. As we have once obtained forgiveness of sins in Baptism, so forgiveness remains day by day as long as we live, that is, as long as we carry the old Adam about our necks.

[5] Cf. Rom. 3:25; Heb. 4:16.

1

What is Holy Communion?

Holy Communion is the body and blood
of our Lord Jesus Christ
given with bread and wine,
instituted by Christ himself
for us to eat and drink.

Where do the Scriptures say this?

Matthew, Mark, Luke, and Paul say:
Our Lord Jesus Christ, in the night in
    which he was betrayed,
took bread; and when he had given thanks,
he broke it and gave it to his disciples,
saying, "Take, eat, this is my body,
    which is given for you;
this do in remembrance of me."

After the same manner also he took the cup
    after supper,
and when he had given thanks,
he gave it to them, saying,
"Drink of it, all of you;
this cup is the new testament in my blood,
which is shed for you, and for many, for the
    remission of sins;
this do, as often as you drink it, in
    remembrance of me."

2

What benefits do we receive from this
sacrament?

The benefits of this sacrament are pointed
    out by the words,
given and shed for you for the remission of
sins.

These words assure us that in the sacrament
we receive forgiveness of sins, life, and
    salvation.
For where there is forgiveness of sins,
there is also life and salvation.

3

How can eating and drinking do all this?

It is not eating and drinking that does this,
but the words, *given and shed for you for
    the remission of sins.*
These words, along with eating and
    drinking, are the main thing in the
        sacrament.
And whoever believes these words
has exactly what they say,
    forgiveness of sins.

4

When is a person rightly prepared to receive this sacrament?

Fasting and other outward preparations
    serve a good purpose.
However, that person is well prepared and
    worthy who believes these words,
*given and shed for you for the remission
    of sins.*
But anyone who does not believe these
    words, or doubts them,
is neither prepared nor worthy,
for the words *for you* require simply
    a believing heart.

As we treated Holy Baptism under three headings, so we must 1
deal with the second sacrament in the same way, stating what it is,
what its benefits are, and who is to receive it. All these are established
from the words by which Christ instituted it. So everyone who 2
wishes to be a Christian and go to the sacrament should be familiar
with them. For we do not intend to admit to the sacrament and
administer it to those who do not know what they seek or why they
come. The words are these:

"Our Lord Jesus Christ on the night when he was betrayed took 3
bread, gave thanks, broke it, and gave it to his disciples and said,
'Take, eat; this is my body, which is given for you. Do this in
remembrance of me.'"

"In the same way also he took the cup, after supper, gave thanks,
and gave it to them, saying, 'This cup is the new testament in my
blood, which is poured out for you for the forgiveness of sins. Do this,
as often as you drink it, in remembrance of me.'" [6]

We have no wish on this occasion to quarrel and dispute with 4
those who blaspheme and desecrate this sacrament; but as in the case
of Baptism, we shall first learn what is of greatest importance, namely,
God's Word and ordinance or command, which is the chief thing
to be considered. For the Lord's Supper was not invented or devised
by any man. It was instituted by Christ without man's counsel or
deliberation. Therefore, just as the Ten Commandments, the 5
Lord's Prayer, and the Creed retain their nature and value even if we
never keep, pray, or believe them, so also does this blessed sacrament
remain unimpaired and inviolate even if we use and handle it unworthily. Do you think God cares so much about our faith and 6
conduct that he would permit them to affect his ordinance? No, all
temporal things remain as God has created and ordered them, regardless
of how we treat them. This must always be emphasized, for thus 7
we can thoroughly refute all the babbling of the seditious spirits who
regard the sacraments, contrary to the Word of God, as human
performances.

Now, what is the Sacrament of the Altar? Answer: It is the 8
true body and blood of the Lord Christ in and under the bread and
wine which we Christians are commanded by Christ's word to eat and
drink. As we said of Baptism that it is not mere water, so we say 9
here that the sacrament is bread and wine, but not mere bread or wine
such as is served at the table. It is bread and wine comprehended in
God's Word and connected with it.

It is the Word, I maintain, which distinguishes it from mere 10
bread and wine and constitutes it a sacrament which is rightly called
Christ's body and blood. It is said, *"Accedat verbum ad elementum et*

---

[6] I Cor. 11:23-25; Matt. 26:26-28; Mark 14:22-24; Luke 22:19f.

fit sacramentum," that is, "When the Word is joined to the external element, it becomes a sacrament." [7] This saying of St. Augustine is so accurate and well put that it is doubtful if he has said anything better. The Word must make the element a sacrament; otherwise it remains a mere element. Now, this is not the word and ordinance of a   11 prince or emperor, but of the divine Majesty at whose feet every knee should bow and confess that it is as he says and should accept it with all reverence, fear, and humility.

With this Word you can strengthen your conscience and declare: 12 "Let a hundred thousand devils, with all the fanatics, rush forward and say, 'How can bread and wine be Christ's body and blood?' Still I know that all the spirits and scholars put together have less wisdom than the divine Majesty has in his little finger. Here we have   13 Christ's word, 'Take, eat; this is my body.' 'Drink of it, all of you, this is the new covenant in my blood,' etc. Here we shall take our stand and see who dares to instruct Christ and alter what he has spoken. It is true, indeed, that if you take the Word away from   14 the elements or view them apart from the Word, you have nothing but ordinary bread and wine. But if the words remain, as is right and necessary, then in virtue of them they are truly the body and blood of Christ. For as we have it from the lips of Christ, so it is; he cannot lie or deceive."

Hence it is easy to answer all kinds of questions which now   15 trouble men — for example, whether even a wicked priest can administer the sacrament, and like questions. Our conclusion is: 16 Even though a knave should receive or administer it, it is the true sacrament (that is, Christ's body and blood) just as truly as when one uses it most worthily. For it is not founded on the holiness of men but on the Word of God. As no saint on earth, yes, no angel in heaven can transform bread and wine into Christ's body and blood, so likewise no one can change or alter the sacrament, even if it is misused. For the Word by which it was constituted a sacrament is not   17 rendered false because of an individual's unworthiness or unbelief. Christ does not say, "If you believe, or if you are worthy, you receive my body and blood," but, "Take, eat and drink, this is my body and blood." Likewise, he says, "Do this," namely, what I now do, what I institute, what I give you and bid you take. This is as much as to   18 say, "No matter whether you are unworthy or worthy, you here have Christ's body and blood by virtue of these words which are coupled with the bread and wine." Mark this and remember it well. For   19 upon these words rest our whole argument, protection, and defense against all errors and deceptions that have ever arisen or may yet arise.

---

[7] Cf. above. IV. Baptism, 18.

We have briefly considered the first part, namely, the essence   20
of this sacrament. Now we come to its power and benefit, the purpose
for which the sacrament was really instituted, for it is most necessary
that we know what we should seek and obtain there. This is   21
plainly evident from the words just quoted, "This is my body and
blood, given and poured out *for you* for the forgiveness of sins."
In other words, we go to the sacrament because we receive there   22
a great treasure, through and in which we obtain the forgiveness of
sins. Why? Because the words are there through which this is imparted!
Christ bids me eat and drink in order that the sacrament may be mine
and may be a source of blessing to me as a sure pledge and sign—
indeed, as the very gift he has provided for me against my sins, death,
and all evils.

Therefore, it is appropriately called the food of the soul since   23
it nourishes and strengthens the new man. While it is true that
through Baptism we are first born anew, our human flesh and blood
have not lost their old skin. There are so many hindrances and
temptations of the devil and the world that we often grow weary and
faint, at times even stumble. The Lord's Supper is given as a   24
daily food and sustenance so that our faith may refresh and strengthen
itself and not weaken in the struggle but grow continually stronger.
For the new life should be one that continually develops and   25
progresses. Meanwhile it must suffer much opposition. The devil   26
is a furious enemy; when he sees that we resist him and attack the
old man, and when he cannot rout us by force, he sneaks and skulks
about everywhere, trying all kinds of tricks, and does not stop until
he has finally worn us out so that we either renounce our faith or yield
hand and foot and become indifferent or impatient. For such   27
times, when our heart feels too sorely pressed, this comfort of the
Lord's Supper is given to bring us new strength and refreshment.

Here again our clever spirits contort themselves with their   28
great learning and wisdom, bellowing and blustering, "How can bread
and wine forgive sins or strengthen faith?" Yet they know that we do
not claim this of bread and wine—since in itself bread is bread—but of
that bread and wine which are Christ's body and blood and with which
the words are coupled. These and no other, we say, are the treasure
through which forgiveness is obtained. This treasure is conveyed   29
and communicated to us in no other way than through the words,
"given and poured out for you." Here you have both truths, that it is
Christ's body and blood and that these are yours as your treasure and
gift. Christ's body can never be an unfruitful, vain thing, impotent   30
and useless. Yet, however great the treasure may be in itself, it must be
comprehended in the Word and offered to us through the Word,
otherwise we could never know of it or seek it.

Therefore it is absurd to say that Christ's body and blood are   31 not given and poured out for us in the Lord's Supper and hence that we cannot have forgiveness of sins in the sacrament. Although the work was accomplished and forgiveness of sins was acquired on the cross, yet it cannot come to us in any other way than through the Word. How should we know that this has been accomplished and offered to us if it were not proclaimed by preaching, by the oral Word? Whence do they know of forgiveness, and how can they grasp and appropriate it, except by steadfastly believing the Scriptures and the Gospel? Now, the whole Gospel and the article of the Creed, "I 32 believe in the holy Christian church, the forgiveness of sins," are embodied in this sacrament and offered to us through the Word. Why, then, should we allow this treasure to be torn out of the sacrament? Our opponents[8] must still confess that these are the very words which we hear everywhere in the Gospel. They can say that these words in the sacrament are of no value just as little as they dare say that the whole Gospel or Word of God apart from the sacrament is of no value.

So far we have treated the sacrament from the standpoint both 33 of its essence and of its effect and benefit. It remains for us to consider who it is that receives this power and benefit. Briefly, as we said above concerning Baptism and in many other places, the answer is: It is he who believes what the words say and what they give, for they are not spoken or preached to stone and wood but to those who hear them, those to whom Christ says, "Take and eat," etc. And 34 because he offers and promises forgiveness of sins, it cannot be received except by faith. This faith he himself demands in the Word when he says, "Given *for you*" and "poured out *for you*," as if he said, "This is why I give it and bid you eat and drink, that you may take it as your own and enjoy it." Whoever lets these words be addressed 35 to him and believes that they are true has what the words declare. But he who does not believe has nothing, for he lets this gracious blessing be offered to him in vain and refuses to enjoy it. The treasure is opened and placed at everyone's door, yes, upon everyone's table, but it is also your responsibility to take it and confidently believe that it is just as the words tell you.

This, now, is the preparation required of a Christian for 36 receiving this sacrament worthily. Since this treasure is fully offered in the words, it can be grasped and appropriated only by the heart. Such a gift and eternal treasure cannot be seized with the hand. Fasting and prayer and the like may have their place as an 37 external preparation and children's exercise so that one's body may behave properly and reverently toward the body and blood of Christ. But what is given in and with the sacrament cannot be grasped and

[8] Zwinglians and Anabaptists.

appropriated by the body. This is done by the faith of the heart which discerns and desires this treasure.

Enough has been said now for all ordinary instruction on the   38 essentials of this sacrament. What may further be said about it belongs to another occasion.

In conclusion, now that we have the right interpretation and   39 doctrine of the sacrament, there is great need also of an admonition and entreaty that so great a treasure, which is daily administered and distributed among Christians, may not be heedlessly passed by. What I mean is that those who claim to be Christians should prepare themselves to receive this blessed sacrament frequently. For we see   40 that men are becoming listless and lazy about its observance. A lot of people who hear the Gospel, now that the pope's nonsense has been abolished and we are freed from his oppression and authority, let a year, or two, three, or more years go by without receiving the sacrament, as if they were such strong Christians that they have no need of it. Some let themselves be kept and deterred from it   41 because we have taught that no one should go unless he feels a hunger and thirst impelling him to it. Some pretend that it is a matter of liberty, not of necessity, and that it is enough if they simply believe. Thus the majority go so far that they become quite barbarous, and ultimately despise both the sacrament and the Word of God.

Now it is true, we repeat, that no one should under any   42 circumstances be coerced or compelled, lest we institute a new slaughter of souls. Nevertheless, let it be understood that people who abstain and absent themselves from the sacrament over a long period of time are not to be considered Christians. Christ did not institute it to be treated merely as a spectacle, but commanded his Christians to eat and drink and thereby remember him.

Indeed, true Christians who cherish and honor the sacrament   43 will of their own accord urge and impel themselves to come. However, in order that the common people and the weak, who also would like to be Christians, may be induced to see the reason and the need for receiving the sacrament, we shall devote a little attention to this point. As in other matters pertaining to faith, love, and patience it is   44 not enough simply to teach and instruct, but there must also be daily exhortation, so on this subject we must be persistent in preaching, lest people become indifferent and bored. For we know from experience that the devil always sets himself against this and every other Christian activity, hounding and driving people from it as much as he can.

In the first place, we have a clear text in the words of Christ,   45 "*Do this* in remembrance of me." These are words of precept and command, enjoining all who would be Christians to partake of the sacrament. They are words addressed to disciples of Christ; hence whoever would be one of them, let him faithfully hold to this sacra-

ment, not from compulsion, coerced by men, but to obey and please
the Lord Christ. However, you may say, "But the words are   46
added, 'as often as you do it'; so he compels no one, but leaves it to
our free choice." I answer: That is true, but it does not say that   47
we should never partake. Indeed, the very words, "as often as you do
it," imply that we should do it often. And they are added because
Christ wishes the sacrament to be free, not bound to a special time
like the Passover, which the Jews were obliged to eat only once a year,
precisely on the evening of the fourteenth day of the first full moon,[9]
without variation of a single day. Christ means to say: "I institute a
Passover or Supper for you, which you shall enjoy not just on this one
evening of the year, but frequently, whenever and wherever you will,
according to everyone's opportunity and need, being bound to no
special place or time" (although the pope afterward perverted it   48
and turned it back into a Jewish feast).[1]

Thus you see that we are not granted liberty to despise the   49
sacrament. When a person, with nothing to hinder him, lets a long
period of time elapse without ever desiring the sacrament, I call that
despising it. If you want such liberty, you may just as well take the
further liberty not to be a Christian; then you need not believe or pray,
for the one is just as much Christ's commandment as the other. But
if you wish to be a Christian, you must from time to time satisfy and
obey this commandment. For this commandment should ever   50
move you to examine your inner life and reflect: "See what sort of
Christian I am! If I were one, I would surely have at least a little
longing to do what my Lord has commanded me to do."

Indeed, since we show such an aversion toward the sacrament,   51
men can easily sense what sort of Christians we were under the papacy
when we attended the sacrament merely from compulsion and fear of
men's commandments, without joy and love and even without regard
for Christ's commandment. But we neither force nor compel   52
anyone, nor need anyone partake of the sacrament to serve or please
us. What should move and impel you is the fact that Christ desires it,
and it pleases him. You should not let yourself be forced by men
either to faith or to any good work. All we are doing is to urge you
to do what you ought to do, not for our sake but for your own. He
invites and incites you; if you despise this, you must answer for it
yourself.

This is the first point, especially for the benefit of the cold and   53
indifferent, that they may come to their senses and wake up. It is
certainly true, as I have found in my own experience, and as everyone

---

[9] Lev. 23:5.

[1] Cf. Fourth Lateran Council (1215): "receiving reverently the sacrament
of the Eucharist at least in Paschal time. . . ." Henry Denzinger, *The Sources
of Catholic Dogma*, tr. R. J. Deferrari (1957), p. 173.

will find in his own case, that if a person stays away from the
sacrament, day by day he will become more and more callous and
cold, and eventually spurn it altogether. To avoid this, we must   54
examine our heart and conscience and act like a person who really
desires to be right with God. The more we do this, the more will our
heart be warmed and kindled, and it will not grow entirely cold.

But suppose you say, "What if I feel that I am unfit?" Answer: 55
This also is my temptation, especially inherited from the old order
under the pope when we tortured ourselves to become so perfectly
pure that God might not find the least blemish in us. Because of this
we became so timid that everyone was thrown into consternation,
saying, "Alas, I am not worthy!" Then nature and reason begin   56
to contrast our unworthiness with this great and precious blessing,
and it appears like a dark lantern in contrast to the bright sun, or as
dung in contrast to jewels. Because nature and reason see this, such
people refuse to go to the sacrament and wait until they become
prepared, until one week passes into another and one half year into
yet another. If you choose to fix your eye on how good and pure   57
you are, to work toward the time when nothing will prick your
conscience, you will never go.

For this reason we must make a distinction among men. Those   58
who are shameless and unruly must be told to stay away, for they
are not fit to receive the forgiveness of sins since they do not desire it
and do not want to be good. The others, who are not so callous   59
and dissolute but would like to be good, should not absent themselves,
even though in other respects they are weak and frail. As St. Hilary
has said, "Unless a man has committed such a sin that he has
forfeited the name of Christian and has to be expelled from the
congregation, he should not exclude himself from the sacrament,"
lest he deprive himself of life.[2] No one will make such progress   60
that he does not retain many common infirmities in his flesh and blood.

People with such misgivings must learn that it is the highest   61
wisdom to realize that this sacrament does not depend upon our
worthiness. We are not baptized because we are worthy and holy,
nor do we come to confession pure and without sin; on the contrary,
we come as poor, miserable men, precisely because we are unworthy.
The only exception is the person who desires no grace and absolution
and has no intention to amend his life.

He who earnestly desires grace and consolation should compel   62
himself to go and allow no one to deter him, saying, "I would really
like to be worthy, but I come not on account of any worthiness of

---

[2] Gratian, *Decretum*, Pt. III, D. 2, c. 15, quotes Hilary: "If a man's sins
are not so great as to require excommunication, he must not exclude himself
from the medicine of the Lord's body." The passage, however, is to be found
in Augustine, Epistle 54, c. 3.

mine, but on account of thy Word, because Thou hast commanded it
and I want to be thy disciple, no matter how insignificant my
worthiness." This is difficult, for we always have this obstacle and   63
hindrance to contend with, that we concentrate more upon ourselves
than upon the words that proceed from Christ's lips. Nature would like
to act in such a way that it may rest and rely firmly upon itself;
otherwise it refuses to take a step. Let this suffice for the first point.

In the second place, a promise is attached to the commandment,   64
as we heard above, which should most powerfully draw and impel us.
Here stand the gracious and lovely words, "This is my body, given
for you," "This is my blood, poured out *for you* for the forgiveness
of sins." These words, I have said, are not preached to wood or   65
stone but to you and me; otherwise Christ might just as well have
kept quiet and not instituted a sacrament. Ponder, then, and include
yourself personally in the "you" so that he may not speak to you in
vain.

In this sacrament he offers us all the treasure he brought from   66
heaven for us, to which he most graciously invites us in other places,
as when he says in Matt. 11:28, "Come to me, all who labor and are
heavy-laden, and I will refresh you." Surely it is a sin and a shame   67
that, when he tenderly and faithfully summons and exhorts us to our
highest and greatest good, we act so distantly toward it, neglecting it
so long that we grow quite cold and callous and lose all desire and
love for it. We must never regard the sacrament as a harmful   68
thing from which we should flee, but as a pure, wholesome, soothing
medicine which aids and quickens us in both soul and body. For
where the soul is healed, the body has benefited also. Why, then,
do we act as if the sacrament were a poison which would kill us if
we ate of it?

Of course, it is true that those who despise the sacrament and   69
lead unchristian lives receive it to their harm and damnation. To
such people nothing can be good or wholesome, just as when a sick
person willfully eats and drinks what is forbidden him by the
physician. But those who feel their weakness, who are anxious to   70
be rid of it and desire help, should regard and use the sacrament as a
precious antidote against the poison in their systems. For here in the
sacrament you receive from Christ's lips the forgiveness of sins, which
contains and conveys God's grace and Spirit with all his gifts,
protection, defense, and power against death and the devil and all evils.

Thus you have on God's part both the commandment and the   71
promise of the Lord Christ. Meanwhile, on your part, you ought to be
impelled by your own need, which hangs around your neck and which
is the very reason for this command and invitation and promise.
Christ himself says, "Those who are well have no need of a physician,

but those who are sick," [3] that is, those who labor and are heavy-laden with sin, fear of death, and the assaults of the flesh and the devil. If you are heavy-laden and feel your weakness, go joyfully to the 72 sacrament and receive refreshment, comfort, and strength. If you 73 wait until you are rid of your burden in order to come to the sacrament purely and worthily, you must stay away from it forever. In such a case Christ pronounces the judgment, "If you are pure 74 and upright, you have no need of me and I have no need of you." Therefore they alone are unworthy who neither feel their infirmities nor admit to being sinners.

Suppose you say, "What shall I do if I cannot feel this need or 75 experience hunger and thirst for the sacrament?" Answer: For persons in such a state of mind that they cannot feel it, I know no better advice than to suggest that they put their hands to their bosom and ask whether they are made of flesh and blood. If you find that you are, then for your own good turn to St. Paul's Epistle to the Galatians and hear what are the fruits of the flesh: "The works of the flesh are plain: adultery, immorality, impurity, licentiousness, idolatry, sorcery, enmity, strife, jealousy, anger, selfishness, dissension, party spirit, envy, murder, drunkenness, carousing, and the like." [4]

If you cannot feel the need, therefore, at least believe the 76 Scriptures. They will not lie to you, and they know your flesh better than you yourself do. Yes, and St. Paul concludes in Rom. 7:18, "For I know that nothing good dwells within me, that is, in my flesh." If St. Paul can speak thus of his flesh, let us not pretend to be better or more holy. But the fact that we are insensitive to our sin is all 77 the worse, for it is a sign that ours is a leprous flesh which feels nothing though the disease rages and rankles. As we have said, 78 even if you are so utterly dead in sin, at least believe the Scriptures, which pronounce this judgment upon you. In short, the less you feel your sins and infirmities, the more reason you have to go to the sacrament and seek a remedy.

Again, look about you and see whether you are also in the 79 world. If you do not know, ask your neighbors about it. If you are in the world, do not think that there will be any lack of sins and needs. Just begin to act as if you want to become good and cling to the Gospel, and see whether you will not acquire enemies who harm, wrong, and injure you and give you occasion for sin and wrong-doing. If you have not experienced this, then take it from the Scriptures, which everywhere give this testimony about the world.

Besides the flesh and the world, you will surely have the devil 80

[3] Matt. 9:12.
[4] Gal. 5:19, 20.

about you. You will not entirely trample him under foot because our Lord Christ himself could not entirely avoid him. Now, what 81 is the devil? Nothing else than what the Scriptures call him, a liar and a murderer.[5] A liar who seduces the heart from God's Word and blinds it, making you unable to feel your needs or come to Christ. A murderer who begrudges you every hour of your life. If you could 82 see how many daggers, spears, and arrows are at every moment aimed at you, you would be glad to come to the sacrament as often as possible. The only reason we go about so securely and heedlessly is that we neither acknowledge nor believe that we are in the flesh, in this wicked world, or under the kingdom of the devil.

Try this, therefore, and practice it well. Just examine yourself, 83 look around a little, cling to the Scriptures. If even then you feel nothing, you have all the more need to lament both to God and to your brother. Take others' advice and seek their prayers, and never give up until the stone is removed from your heart. Then your 84 need will become apparent, and you will perceive that you have sunk twice as low as any other poor sinner and are much in need of the sacrament to combat your misery. This misery, unfortunately, you do not see, though God grants his grace that you may become more sensitive to it and more hungry for the sacrament. This happens especially because the devil so constantly besieges you and lies in wait to trap and destroy you, soul and body, so that you cannot be safe from him one hour. How quickly can he bring you into misery and distress when you least expect it!

Let this serve as an exhortation, then, not only for us who are 85 grown and advanced in years, but also for the young people who ought to be brought up in Christian doctrine and a right understanding of it. With such training we may more easily instill the Ten Commandments, the Creed, and the Lord's Prayer into the young so that they will receive them with joy and earnestness, practice them from their youth, and become accustomed to them. For it is 86 clearly useless to try to change old people. We cannot perpetuate these and other teachings unless we train the people who come after us and succeed us in our office and work, so that they in turn may bring up their children successfully. Thus the Word of God and the Christian church will be preserved. Therefore let every head of a 87 household remember that it is his duty, by God's injunction and command, to teach or have taught to his children the things they ought to know. Since they are baptized and received into the Christian church, they should also enjoy this fellowship of the sacrament so that they may serve us and be useful. For they must all help us to believe, to love, to pray, and to fight the devil.

[5] John 8:44.

THE OFFICE OF THE KEYS

What is the "Office of the Keys"?

It is that authority which Christ gave to his church to forgive the sins of those who repent and to declare to those who do not repent that their sins are not forgiven.

What are the words of Christ?

Our Lord Jesus Christ said to his disciples: "Receive the Holy Spirit. If you forgive the sins of any, they are forgiven; if you retain the sins of any, they are retained."—John 20:23

"Truly, I say to you, whatever you bind on earth shall be bound in heaven, and whatever you loose on earth shall be loosed in heaven."—Matthew 18:18

CONFESSION

What is private confession?

Private confession has two parts. First, we make a personal confession of sins to the pastor, and then we receive absolution, which means forgiveness as from God himself. This absolution we should not doubt, but firmly believe that thereby our sins are forgiven before God in heaven.

What sins should we confess?

Before God we should confess that we are guilty of all sins, even those which are not known to us, as we do in the Lord's Prayer. But in private confession, as before the pastor, we should confess only those sins which trouble us in heart and mind.

What are such sins?

We can examine our everyday life according to the Ten Commandments—for example, how we act toward father or mother, son or daughter, husband or wife, or toward the people with whom we work, and so on. We may ask ourselves whether we have been disobedient or unfaithful, bad-tempered or dishonest, or whether we have hurt anyone by word or deed.

How might we confess our sins privately?

We may say that we wish to confess our sins and to receive absolution in God's name. We may begin by saying, "I, a poor sinner, confess before God that I am guilty of many sins." Then we should name the sins that trouble us. We may close the confession with the words, "I repent of all these sins and pray for mercy. I promise to do better with God's help."

What if we are not troubled by any special sins?

We should not torture ourselves with imaginary sins. If we cannot think of any sins to confess (which would hardly ever happen), we need not name any in particular, but may receive absolution because we have already made a general confession to God.

How may we be assured of forgiveness?

The pastor may pronounce the absolution by saying, "By the authority of our Lord Jesus Christ I forgive you your sins in the name of the Father and of the Son and of the Holy Spirit. Amen."

Those who are heavily burdened in conscience the pastor may comfort and encourage with further assurances from God's Word.

A Brief Exhortation to Confession

Here follows an exhortation to confession.[6]

Concerning confession, we have always taught that it should be   1
voluntary and purged of the pope's tyranny. We have been set free
from his coercion and from the intolerable burden he imposed upon
the Christian church. Up to now, as we all know from experience,
there has been no law quite so oppressive as that which forced
everyone to make confession on pain of the gravest mortal sin.
Moreover, it so greatly burdened and tortured consciences with the   2
enumeration of all kinds of sin that no one was able to confess purely
enough. Worst of all, no one taught or understood what confession   3
is and how useful and comforting it is. Instead, it was made sheer
anguish and a hellish torture since people had to make confession
even though nothing was more hateful to them. These three things   4
have now been removed and made voluntary so that we may confess
without coercion or fear, and we are released from the torture of
enumerating all sins in detail. Moreover, we have the advantage of
knowing how to use confession beneficially for the comforting and
strengthening of our conscience.

Everyone knows this now. Unfortunately, men have learned it   5
only too well; they do whatever they please and take advantage of
their freedom, acting as if they will never need or desire to go to
confession any more. We quickly understand whatever benefits us,
and we grasp with uncommon ease whatever in the Gospel is mild
and gentle. But such pigs, as I have said, are unworthy to appear in
the presence of the Gospel or to have any part of it. They ought
to remain under the pope and submit to being driven and tormented
to confess, fast, etc., more than ever before. For he who will not
believe the Gospel, live according to it, and do what a Christian ought
to do, should enjoy none of its benefits. What would happen if   6
you wished to enjoy the Gospel's benefits but did nothing about it and
paid nothing for it? For such people we shall provide no preaching,
nor will they have our permission to share and enjoy any part of our
liberty, but we shall let the pope or his like bring them back into
subjection and coerce them like the tyrant he is. The rabble who
will not obey the Gospel deserve just such a jailer as God's devil and
hangman. To others who hear it gladly, however, we must always   7
preach, exhorting, encouraging, and persuading them not to lose this
precious and comforting treasure which the Gospel offers. Therefore
we must say something about confession to instruct and admonish the
simple folk.

---

[6] The section on confession was added first in the 1529 revised edition of
the Catechism. It was omitted in the Jena edition of Luther's Works and in
the German Book of Concord, hence also in several later editions of the
Catechism.

To begin with, I have said that in addition to the confession   8
which we are discussing here there are two other kinds, which have an
even greater right to be called the Christians' common confession. I
refer to the practice of confessing to God alone or to our neighbor
alone, begging for forgiveness. These two kinds are expressed in the
Lord's Prayer when we say, "Forgive us our debts, as we forgive our
debtors," etc. Indeed, the whole Lord's Prayer is nothing else than   9
such a confession. For what is our prayer but a confession that we
neither have nor do what we ought and a plea for grace and a happy
conscience? This kind of confession should and must take place
incessantly as long as we live. For this is the essence of a genuinely
Christian life, to acknowledge that we are sinners and to pray for grace.

Similarly the second confession, which each Christian makes   10
toward his neighbor, is included in the Lord's Prayer. We are to
confess our guilt before one another and forgive one another before
we come into God's presence to beg for forgiveness. Now, all of us
are debtors one to another, therefore we should and we may confess
publicly in everyone's presence, no one being afraid of anyone else.
For it is true, as the proverb says, "If one man is upright, so are   11
they all"; no one does to God or his neighbor what he ought.
However, besides our universal guilt there is also a particular one,
when a person has provoked another to anger and needs to beg his
pardon. Thus we have in the Lord's Prayer a twofold absolution: 12
our debts both to God and to our neighbor are forgiven when we
forgive our neighbor and become reconciled with him.

Besides this public, daily, and necessary confession, there is   13
also the secret confession which takes place privately before a single
brother. When some problem or quarrel sets us at one another's
throats and we cannot settle it, and yet we do not find ourselves
sufficiently strong in faith, we may at any time and as often as we wish
lay our complaint before a brother, seeking his advice, comfort, and
strength. This type of confession is not included in the command-   14
ment like the other two but is left to everyone to use whenever he
needs it. Thus by divine ordinance Christ himself has entrusted
absolution to his Christian church and commanded us to absolve one
another from sins.[7] So if there is a heart that feels its sin and desires
consolation, it has here a sure refuge when it hears in God's Word that
through a man God looses and absolves him from his sins.

Note, then, as I have often said, that confession consists of   15
two parts. The first is my work and act, when I lament my sin and
desire comfort and restoration for my soul. The second is a work
which God does, when he absolves me of my sins through a word
placed in the mouth of a man. This is the surpassingly grand and

[7] Matt. 18:15-19.

noble thing that makes confession so wonderful and comforting. In the past we placed all the emphasis on our work alone, and we 16 were only concerned whether we had confessed purely enough. We neither noticed nor preached the very necessary second part; it was just as if our confession were simply a good work with which we could satisfy God. Where the confession was not made perfectly and in complete detail, we were told that the absolution was not valid and the sin was not forgiven. Thereby the people were driven to the 17 point that everyone inevitably despaired of confessing so purely (which was impossible), and nobody could feel his conscience at peace or have confidence in his absolution. Thus the precious confession was not only made useless to us but it also became burdensome and bitter, to the manifest harm and destruction of souls.

We should therefore take care to keep the two parts clearly 18 separate. We should set little value on our work but exalt and magnify God's Word. We should not act as if we wanted to perform a magnificent work to present to him, but simply to accept and receive something from him. You dare not come and say how good or how wicked you are. If you are a Christian, I know this well enough 19 anyway; if you are not, I know it still better. But what you must do is to lament your need and allow yourself to be helped so that you may attain a happy heart and conscience.

Further, no one dare oppress you with requirements. Rather, 20 whoever is a Christian, or would like to be one, has here the faithful advice to go and obtain this precious treasure. If you are no Christian, and desire no such comfort, we shall leave you to another's power. Hereby we abolish the pope's tyranny, commandments, and 21 coercion since we have no need of them. For our teaching, as I have said, is this: If anybody does not go to confession willingly and for the sake of absolution, let him just forget about it. Yes, and if anybody goes about relying on the purity of his confession, let him just stay away from it. We urge you, however, to confess and express your 22 needs, not for the purpose of performing a work but to hear what God wishes to say to you. The Word or absolution, I say, is what you should concentrate on, magnifying and cherishing it as a great and wonderful treasure to be accepted with all praise and gratitude.

If all this were clearly explained, and meanwhile if the needs 23 which ought to move and induce us to confession were clearly indicated, there would be no need of coercion and force. A man's own conscience would impel him and make him so anxious that he would rejoice and act like a poor, miserable beggar who hears that a rich gift, of money or clothes, is to be given out at a certain place; he would need no bailiff to drive and beat him but would run there as fast as he could so as not to miss the gift. Suppose, now, that the invitation were 24 changed into a command that all beggars should run to the place, no reason being given and no mention of what they were to look for or receive. How else would the beggar go but with repugnance, not expecting to receive anything but just letting everyone see how poor and miserable he is? Not much joy or comfort would come from this, but only a greater hostility to the command.

In the same way the pope's preachers have in the past kept   25 silence about this wonderful, rich alms and this indescribable treasure; they have simply driven men together in hordes just to show what impure and filthy people they were. Who could thus go to confession willingly? We, on the contrary, do not say that men should look   26 to see how full of filthiness you are, making of you a mirror for contemplating themselves. Rather we advise: If you are poor and miserable, then go and make use of the healing medicine. He who   27 feels his misery and need will develop such a desire for confession that he will run toward it with joy. But those who ignore it and do not come of their own accord, we let go their way. However, they ought to know that we do not regard them as Christians.

Thus we teach what a wonderful, precious, and comforting   28 thing confession is, and we urge that such a precious blessing should not be despised, especially when we consider our great need. If you are a Christian, you need neither my compulsion nor the pope's command at any point, but you will compel yourself and beg me for the privilege of sharing in it. However, if you despise it and   29 proudly stay away from confession, then we must come to the conclusion that you are no Christian and that you ought not receive the sacrament. For you despise what no Christian ought to despise, and you show thereby that you can have no forgiveness of sin. And this is a sure sign that you also despise the Gospel.

In short, we approve of no coercion. However, if anyone   30 refuses to hear and heed the warning of our preaching, we shall have nothing to do with him, nor may he have any share in the Gospel. If you are a Christian, you should be glad to run more than a hundred miles for confession, not under compulsion but rather coming and compelling us to offer it. For here the compulsion must be   31 inverted; we must come under the command and you must come into freedom. We compel no man, but allow ourselves to be compelled, just as we are compelled to preach and administer the sacrament.

Therefore, when I urge you to go to confession, I am simply   32 urging you to be a Christian. If I bring you to this point, I have also brought you to confession. Those who really want to be good Christians, free from their sins, and happy in their conscience, already have the true hunger and thirst. They snatch at the bread just like a hunted hart, burning with heat and thirst, as Ps. 42:2 says, "As a   33 hart longs for flowing streams, so longs my soul for thee, O God."

That is, as a hart trembles with eagerness for a fresh spring, so I yearn and tremble for God's Word, absolution, the sacrament, etc. In 34 this way, you see, confession would be rightly taught, and such a desire and love for it would be aroused that people would come running after us to get it, more than we would like. We shall let the papists torment and torture themselves and other people who ignore such a treasure and bar themselves from it. As for ourselves, however, let us lift our 35 hands in praise and thanks to God that we have attained to this blessed knowledge of confession.